Trip-Hop

A 33⅓ SERIES

Forthcoming in *Genre: A 33 1/3 Series*

Trip-Hop

R.J. Wheaton

BLOOMSBURY ACADEMIC
NEW YORK • LONDON • OXFORD • NEW DELHI • SYDNEY

BLOOMSBURY ACADEMIC
Bloomsbury Publishing Inc
1385 Broadway, New York, NY 10018, USA
50 Bedford Square, London, WC1B 3DP, UK
29 Earlsfort Terrace, Dublin 2, Ireland

BLOOMSBURY, BLOOMSBURY ACADEMIC and the Diana logo
are trademarks of Bloomsbury Publishing Plc

First published in the United States of America 2023

Library of Congress Cataloging-in-Publication Data
Names: Wheaton, R. J., author.
Title: Trip-hop / R.J. Wheaton.
Description: New York : Bloomsbury Academic, 2022. |
Series: Genre: a 33 1/3 series | Includes bibliographical references and index. |
Summary: "Guides readers through the genre of trip-hop as the first book on
the genre in 20 years, right at a time when trip-hop is making a revival in both
underground scenes and popular artists"– Provided by publisher.
Identifiers: LCCN 2022014603 (print) | LCCN 2022014604 (ebook) |
ISBN 9781501373602 (paperback) | ISBN 9781501373619 (epub) |
ISBN 9781501373626 (pdf) | ISBN 9781501373633
Subjects: LCSH: Trip-hop (Music)–History and criticism.
Classification: LCC ML3540.5 .W54 2022 (print) | LCC ML3540.5 (ebook) |
DDC 781.648–dc23/eng/20220506
LC record available at https://lccn.loc.gov/2022014603
LC ebook record available at https://lccn.loc.gov/2022014604

ISBN: PB: 978-1-5013-7360-2
       ePDF: 978-1-5013-7362-6
       eBook: 978-1-5013-7361-9

Series: Genre: A 33 1/3 Series

Typeset by Integra Software Services Pvt. Ltd.
Printed and bound in Great Britain

To find out more about our authors and books visit
www.bloomsbury.com and sign up for our newsletters.

Contents

Prologue: Beat Bop

One way to think about trip-hop is 1982.

'Buffalo Gals', a single by Malcolm McLaren and the World's Famous Supreme Team, cracked the top 10 in the UK that year. McLaren, former manager of the New York Dolls and the Sex Pistols, had the idea after seeing an Afrika Bambaataa block party. The song was a weird hip-hop-meets-square-dancing cover of an old American minstrelsy song.

In Leeds, in northern England, George Evelyn – later of Nightmares on Wax – remembered that first contact with hip-hop:

> It come like a lightning bolt, bam, it was like wow, scratching, breakdancing, rapping, graffiti all in one video. It was like from another planet. That hit every one of us, everybody in our neighbourhood. I remember going to school the morning after *Top of the Pops*, that Friday morning, and everyone was trying to break and pop in the school yard. It was like everybody had been hit with this tidal wave of something, we just didn't know what it was.

The hip-hop film *Wild Style* was completed in 1982. Ishi Hideaki, then twenty-one and still drifting into a life of delinquency, would see it in Tokyo – 'it totally did a number on me'. He was inspired by hip-hop's two-turntables-and-a-microphone technique: two copies of the same record played in relay to extend an instrumental 'breakbeat', while an MC rapped on top. In the years ahead, as DJ

Krush, he would dig for obscure records 'until my hands turned black. I would shop until I used up all of my change to ride the train, and had to walk home from Shinjuku.'

Wild Style would take hip-hop's culture – rapping (MC'ing), DJ'ing, graffiti (writing) and breakdancing – all over the world. In Bristol, in southwest England, Miles Johnson (DJ Milo), Grant Marshall (Daddy G) and Nellee Hooper were then playing house parties and would soon begin a series of Wednesdays at the Dug Out Club. As the core of a loose collective known as the Wild Bunch, they would play a mix of reggae, dub, Lovers Rock, punk and hip-hop on towering sound systems and at their club nights.

In a hotel room in Rome in 1982, African-American artist Jean-Michel Basquiat sketched fashion model Leslie Winer – later to be called 'the grandmother of trip-hop'. Basquiat was already famous: his second Italian solo exhibition was held that year. Just a few years earlier, as part of SAMO, he had been painting graffiti in Lower Manhattan. In the work of artists like DONDI, Blade, Daze, Futura 2000 and Rammellzee, graffiti was a celebration of creativity, ingenuity and daring on vertiginous overpasses and reachless rooftops, a declaration of right of access to railyards and tunnels, and the creation of imagined communities wherever a subway car might reach.

In Basquiat's sketch, Winer is reading a magazine in bed. The sketch features the numbers 337–5537 in the corner.

> I lived with him mostly off and sometimes on for a couple of years … 3375537 is my name upside-down, calculator-wise, phone-number length. Basquiat used it for tagging. Dondi White and Rammellzee would use it as far north as the Bronx as what I like to call a 'fat-girl nod' in my direction.

Not long afterwards, Basquiat produced (and designed the cover art for) a 500-copy release of 'Beat Bop', a record by Rammellzee and K-Rob. Rammellzee – *Gothic Futurist*, not graffiti artist – had rapped in *Wild Style*'s climactic scene. 'Nobody made records like that', said Cory Robbins, who re-released it later (without Basquiat artwork). 'It was druggy, it was so out there. All of a sudden there's lots of echo, and then the echo's gone'. For writer Greg Tate it was 'a sighing, whinnying ambient shuffle full of funk and suspense that creeps through your head like a slow-moving ghost train'. On 'Beat Bop', Tate heard 'Ramm's oblique streaks of surreal verbiage suggest William S. Burroughs doing cut-ups on acid'.

And in London, a teenage Gilles Peterson DJ'd a stand-in gig at the Electric Ballroom in Camden. 'The best dancers were up there, like the dons of the scene at the time.' The room was the pinnacle of the underground UK jazz dance scene: acrobatic, intricate, virtuosic, joyous; a relentlessly competitive celebration of Black excellence, innovation and heritage. Peterson told Mark 'Snowboy' Cotgrove 'It was the most daunting and delusioning DJ gig I'd ever had. I was scared shitless. I'm this little white kid, and they're thinking, "What are you doing, doing the big man's job?"' He cleared the floor.

1 Trip-hop

One way to think about trip-hop is as one of the 1990s' most revealing bad ideas. DJ Shadow's 'In/Flux' came out in 1993 on London's Mo' Wax label, billed as 'subtle, subliminal and elusive to define'.

Writing about the record for dance and electronic music magazine *Mixmag* the following June, Andy Pemberton defined it:

> This is trip hop, a deft fusion of head-nodding beats, supa-phat bass and an obsessive attention to the kind of other-worldly sounds usually found on acid house records. It comes from the suburbs, not the streets, and with no vocals you don't need to be American to make it sound convincing. All you need are crazy beats and fucked up sounds and you've got the most exciting thing to happen to hip-hop in a long time. Right now there are bedroom homeboys making innovative, tripped out hip-hop that is nothing like the US blueprint of slamming beats and cunning rhymes.

The term tailed back to acid jazz, and – before it – acid house. 'It's like taking acid at a hip-hop gig', wrote Pemberton. Acid hip-hop? Trip-hop.

People hated it from the start.

'Stop categorizing shit!' responded Mo' Wax founder James Lavelle. Kevin Foakes who as Strictly Kev was a longtime designer for the Ninja Tune label and member of DJ Food – also despaired of it. 'Oh how I groaned when I first heard the phrase', he recalled.

So obvious, cheesy and naff … How I lament what the name came to represent: downtempo, 'blunted' beat workouts with no direction, the same clichéd phrases copped from golden era Hip Hop tracks repeated throughout ad infinitum. The relentless thud of the snare on the 2 and 4 of the bar, a 'jazzy' horn sample looped endlessly …

The term became associated with acts from Bristol, including Massive Attack, Portishead, Tricky, and duo Smith & Mighty. Rob Smith remembered a gig at London's Shepherd's Bush Empire:

When Tricky came onstage, he asked the crowd, 'Who likes trip hop?' Some people cheered and shouted 'Yeah!' and Tricky replied, 'Well, fuck off home then!'

But the term 'trip-hop' was memorable and practical – not least because the music was so broad and diverse that no one could agree on what it meant. Looking back in a 2018 documentary about Mo' Wax, graphic designer Ian Swift – Swifty – recalled 'What people called trip-hop: hip-hop, soul, reggae vibe, slowing down of the beats, for the head-nodders, for the stoners'. *Rolling Stone*, catching up in 1996, said 'trip-hop replaces rapping with a head-tripping spaciness, creating a sound in which hip-hop, experimental rock, jazz, ambient and techno vibrantly co-exist'. Later, looking back, Strictly Kev could still see the breadth of the moment:

'Trip Hop' (my definition) – Essentially psychedelic beat collages, usually instrumental, embracing samples, analogue electronics and dub FX. Largely dispensing with the ego of the vocalist in favour of spoken word, incorporating found sounds, fuzz and the most banging drums ever recorded.

Questing, otherworldly and intent of taking the listener (*user?*) on a trip of the most lysergic kind … An amazing mess of styles, soundscapes and head trips

Another way to think about trip-hop is 'classic British marketing from the media', in the words of DJ Gilles Peterson. When Tricky's debut album *Maxinquaye* came out, in 1995, Julian Palmer (A&R for label 4th & Broadway) remembered that the term 'definitely helped. Call it a scene with a catchy name, and everybody buys into it'. Even though most of the artists loathed the term, it was useful enough to the music industry to stick around, briefly, just long enough to generate new music in its form. And then it was formulaic, and so it was swept away. Today it seems an inert genre, one of several not-at-all-missed terms: IDM, electronica, folktronica. For some people – you can argue about it on Reddit – it is a precise term of art and time: particular artists, particular labels, during particular years; for others, just torch songs with beats, or a dull blur of background lounge music.

In that regard the 'blunted' jazzy instrumental hip-hop that became background music at hotel bars and clothing boutiques, a use hated by most of the artists who made it – trip-hop is all around us. I write this in 2022, with the 'chillhop' or 'lo-fi' beats of TikTok home tours and of YouTube study mixes with anime-inspired GIFs – not to mention innumerable 'chill beats to quarantine to' playlists. And, as Gilles Peterson suggests, 'A lot of what you call bass music today could easily have been called trip-hop back then, can still be called trip-hop right now. It's just a term to help focus people's attention on a certain type of sound.'

Certainly, the many artists today making thrilling and interesting music at the intersections of electronic music and hip-hop and dub and jazz won't use the words 'trip-hop' to describe their sound – even if they *are* influenced by albums like Massive Attack's *Mezzanine*, Portishead's *Dummy*, Tricky's *Maxinquaye*, DJ Shadow's *Endtroducing .....*, or the artists on Ninja Tune's mid-1990s' roster, or on one of Mo' Wax's gargantuan *Headz* compilations. Or even if, like those artists, their work exists in the continuum that made New York's 'illbient' scene from the same raw materials; the same continuum that leads through the 2000s LA beat scene; and through the 2010s jazz scenes in London and elsewhere. Trip-hop's minimalism was a remarkably supple template that could accommodate itself to vocal styles and musics around the world. But that didn't necessarily mean coherence or influence, or that there was really a trip-hop there.

As DJ Shadow said years later, 'It's not like you could sit down and write on a piece of paper "Okay here's the lineage". Because, it just doesn't work that way in music. And plus, just geographically we were all over the place.'

Another way to think about trip-hop is how the spaces changed. The spaces changed from underground clubs and warehouses and shebeens and house parties to chill-out rooms in commercial clubs and the arches beneath railways and modish nightclubs, and then to boutiques and coffeeshops and airport lounges and then to elevators and the reception areas at real estate agent offices, and along the way to student dorms and bedrooms and to headphones.

Trip-hop was an unstable compound of dub, hip-hop, ambient house, Lovers Rock or soul or R&B, and of jazz, sort of. It was so in part because it inherited the spaces in which those musics were created and heard. From the soundsystems built, dissembled and re-built by Jamaican immigrants to Britain from the 1960s and 1970s; from the cavernous throb of Berlin techno at the frontiers of ideological collapse in the 1990s; to the intimacy of Lovers Rock at a blues dance; and the nightclub performances of jazz lounge singers. As the music changed the spaces changed with it; or, as higher rents and gentrification and 'quality of life' came to Manhattan and East London, trip-hop became associated with a bourgeois lifestylism. And even as the music could – at best – still retain something of the cavern and the boudoir, you were more likely to hear it in the coffeeshop or the boutique.

And so another way to think about trip-hop is in the change of imagined communities: what listeners in those spaces could understand of the community that the music formed around them. From those finding refuge in music from violence, police, racism; to ravers in collective revolt against a lifetime of 9-to-5; to dancers in intimate swoon; to *consumers,* digital nomads, developers developers developers. From subalterns to students. Trip-hop moved from public spaces to private. From collective consciousness, emergent, losing yourself in a crowd; to getting fucked up and coming down; to deliverance beneath your headphones: 'dance music for your head'.

Another way to think about trip-hop is as a kind of aural gentrification, operating at one edge of hip-hop's rise to global culture. Much of what was wrong with the idea of trip-hop was present in that first article for *Mixmag*. The suggestion that hip-hop had somehow been improved; that the improvement had come 'from the suburbs, not the streets'. That it had been achieved 'with original sounds previously unheard of' – setting aside hip-hop's long and rich instrumental tradition; and as if it had not been locked for years in legal and intergenerational fights about whether it was allowed to sound at all.

As I was writing this book, I had an informal subtitle in mind: *how music forgets*. Not, how music has forgotten trip-hop: this book is not an attempt to restore to the term a repute it never held. But rather, how trip-hop was an *instrument* of forgetting: how, presented as a new new thing, it obscured much of its origins, and how categorization of this type becomes a means to replace some people's voices with those of others. Morcheeba's Paul Godfrey suggested in 1997 that the term 'trip-hop' 'insults the term "hip hop". … You're dealing with middle class people who can afford the equipment to make hip-hop but don't know any rappers'.

Categories encode hierarchy, disallow chance and obscure wonder. If trip-hop was a thing, then it was also to say that dub's range could not accommodate a Massive Attack or a Smith & Mighty; nor hip-hop's a DJ Shadow or DJ Krush. And trip-hop, with its roots in *multiple* musics of Black origin, became part of a larger, and still shameful, architecture through which electronic and dance musics were denuded of their Black (and queer) origins.

And finally, one way to think about trip-hop is in memory of Netscape Navigator. Trip-hop might seem to us a rusty, parochial pre-Internet genre – well past its creative peak by the time the

MP3, Napster and the iPod punctured the music industry's 1990s CD revenue balloon. But trip-hop was coincident, almost exactly, with the rise and fall of the first widely popular web browser, whose rapid feature evolution and stop-start version-to-version changes and all-nighter hacks and workarounds were what made it interesting and wild – and ultimately too unstable for the commercial potentialities of broadband. If trip-hop's rise and fall was a small eddy between two giant global cultural vortices – hip-hop and Internet distribution – it can nonetheless tell us something about what happens when musics are uncoupled from place; when 'new genres' are brought into being more by arbiters than by musicians and audiences; when listeners have uneven access to the music of the past; how music evolves when its constraints shift from being about physical distribution to intellectual property. All these questions, obviously, are Internet questions – and no less present now than they were then.

Genres stick where they solve problems, offer shorthands ('sort of like dub, and hip-hop but without rapping, and sometimes also singing?') and create social capital for labels or promoters or those in the know. They are instruments of precarity, too: a means to administer limited airplay and recognition. And trip-hop certainly was this. It got into artists' heads. DJ Shadow's debut full-length album *Endtroducing.....* came out in 1996, *after* Portishead's *Dummy* and Tricky's *Maxinquaye.* He worried that 'I had missed the boat by not ... sort of beating everybody else to the punch':

> I think we were buying some of the hype that *NME* and *Melody Maker* were spinning .... 'Oh maybe we *are* competing with these other groups.' ... There was a little bit of 'we're not all going to make it out of these alive.'

That precarity was informed in the 1990s – as it still is, obviously – by race; and as we'll see, trip-hop was so often a means to occlude musics of Black origin. To be sure, trip-hop included many multiracial groups and biracial or Black artists. And for the most part white artists approached this music's Black origins with reverence, though that wasn't always the same as respect, and it certainly wasn't the same as reward. I wrote this book mindful of how treacherous a frame is trip-hop to examining those questions, and how particular is the perspective that I bring to it. I wrote this book as a white listener for whom the attention that trip-hop received in the 1990s fuelled an intoxication with hip-hop and jazz. But I write this now – an archivist of sorts – aiming to suggest a few themes that hang it together, and some of the music's 'roots' as it branches, still, into the future. Neither of those perspectives is sufficient to out-think the shortcomings and compromises of the other.

So this book isn't a comprehensive release guide, nor an effort to reanimate a term that started in disrepute and ended in disrepair. The most obvious records are suggested by big-platform algorithms and playlists; the most obscure by Reddit threads. Artist biographies can be easily found, nowadays, on Wikipedia or on twenty-year anniversary oral histories.

This book aims to add context to the music. I have avoided casting 'trip-hop' in inverted commas, or sneering at 'so-called trip-hop', which suggest a futile attempt to pretend the term wasn't used, or to faintly disparage the quality of so much of this music, unfairly tagged with a lousy name. Instead, the project of this book is to complicate the picture a bit: to examine the music's ragged edges – at its start, its end, and its boundaries. I hope it is duly respectful of the experiences of dislocation, contingency, nostalgia, search – and joy – characteristic of this music at its best, and broadest.

For the most part this book keeps its frame to the 1990s and early 2000s (even where some of the same artists released excellent music later on). Exceptions are intended to unsettle boundaries or suggest continuities across them. Some recommendations may veer sometimes more towards the unexpected. If there was plenty of lounge chum in this music – there was – I've tried to only include the best of it in this book. The algorithms will certainly provide the rest. (Though, if you can afford it, the music's artists – and its dynamic range – will be better served by purchasing, on platforms like Bandcamp, where a number of this book's less-known recommendations have recently become available.)

This book is necessarily fragmentary – so many of the records are not only half forgotten but were also imperfect, unfinished and delayed. There were gaps in what was *made* available: even a casual glance will note the under-representation of female producers, for example. Where producers like Neotropic or leila made some of the best albums in this genre, they received less attention than their due; and in the pervasive sexism of 1990s electronic music industry we can never know the many unsigned artists whose music was never brought to a wider public.

Categories seem to us merely descriptive when they are crafted along divisions that it is societally mandated or commercially useful for us to look away from: early blues and early country; blues and early rock & roll. In the manner of all ideology, they seem inevitable, *natural*.

This is another way of saying that categories like trip-hop confirm – *ratify* – the systems that present them. And we forgive ourselves in not noticing this because taste seems so subjective to us: something we arrive at ourselves, not via media 'gatekeepers' or platform algorithms.

Perhaps we have a responsibility to challenge these categories, or at least to corrode their neat edges. I hope there is enough in this book to engage the curiosity of the listener. Curiosity is where it starts.

2 Dub-hop

*Soundsystems – dub – diaspora – Mad Professor – Berlin &
dub techno*

'It comes from the suburbs, not the streets' claimed Andy
Pemberton, coining the term trip-hop. That was a stretch:
it came from London, Bristol, New York, Paris. But if the
metaphor can be stretched to suggest conformity, and racial
gerrymandering, perhaps it was appropriate for what was to
come. In fairness it conveyed, too, how much the acoustic
world of suburban England was changing. I grew up a white kid
on the outskirts of London. Every fifteen minutes there was an
aural reminder, in the passing trains, of the shared timetables
and the commuter newspapers: the mechanics of the nation
state's 'imagined community', in Benedict Anderson's phrase,
still then in its default assumptions of white English identity.

And yet the stray radio signals from London conveyed –
even to listeners like me, outsiders to Black culture – the
possibility of a different frame of reference; even as it was
doused in the static as ever-present as the insect life still then
thick in the long summer nights.

Above all: *bass*. Even if, as a teenager in 1980s, 1990s England
you hadn't scrambled over hedgerow thicket or wire to get to
a rave on farms, commons, on moors, you had probably *heard*
one. Raves were part of the long diffusion into British music of
Jamaica soundsystem culture – bass culture.

'The soundsystem was reggae's radio', said British dub pioneer Dennis Bovell. In Jamaica, the first soundsystems had begun to replace live dance bands in the 1950s, playing music in dancehalls or outdoors. They were in ferocious competition for listeners, labels scratched from records to hide the names of tracks from rivals.

The first UK soundsystems followed closely the first post-war immigrants from Jamaica. The soundsystems were to take on a crucial role in Black community, competition, innovation, youth, heritage. Soundsystems offered a nightlife experience for Black communities excluded from licensed clubs and pubs by the era's rampant 'entrance apartheid', as writer Lloyd Bradley puts it. They were a way to discover and break music from Jamaica and from the UK.

Soundsystems were deeply contested by police and the white population through the post-war decades. The 1980 film *Babylon* (its score by Dennis Bovell) vividly dramatized the role of soundsystems against the backdrop of racism, of social and economic exclusion and of precarity of young Black life. The film was given an X rating to limit its circulation.[1] With that context it was remarkable that – as we'll see – by the early 1990s thick basslines were, in musics descended from and related to reggae, resounding in long wavelengths across the English countryside where, not many decades earlier, the bass tones of gargantuan church organs had illustrated a very different sonic order.

'Reggae had a bottom end, we used to say', recalled Mykaell Riley of UK roots reggae band Steel Pulse, contrasting it with the mastered–for–radio midrange of American funk and R&B. 'In the UK we weren't *on* radio anywhere so it didn't make any difference. So we're mixing for the sound system. It *must* sound good on the sound. On big speakers. It must move you physically.'

These were basslines 'sounding like power lines being strummed across huge electric pylons', said Mark Stewart of The Pop Group – whose music would combine punk raw impetuousness and radical politics with a bass-heavy variant of reggae that emerged from Jamaica in the 1970s: dub.

'Dub plates' were cheap acetate recordings pressed to preview new material as the Jamaican soundsystems of the early 1970s competed with one another. Studio engineers produced exclusive mixes – sometimes even with vocal call-out 'specials'. Soundsystem selectors discovered that with instrumental 'drum & bass'[2] versions they could create and release tension, give an audience space to sing the vocals and allow a deejay to 'toast', or vocalize to energize the crowd.

With songs stripped down to the drum and bass parts, as Michael Veal puts it, 'chords could now be as easily used as bits of abstract color and texture'. The classic dub albums began to appear in 1973, like Lee Perry's *Upsetters 14 Dub Blackboard Jungle* with King Tubby, or Herman Chin Loy's *Aquarius Dub*, or Clive Chin's *Java Java Dub*. They revealed an extraordinary terrain for improvisation, not by musicians and vocalists, but by the engineer in the studio.

Original dub producers like King Tubby, Sylvan Morris, Errol Thompson, Clive Chin and Lee 'Scratch' Perry stripped records down to their elements, subjecting them to effects, filtering, decay, reverberation, slowing and weathering, changing their tonal and textural character; clouding them with accidental or artificial noise; using false starts; and bringing them back in and again out of the mix.

Dub is spatial music. Records are soaked in reverberation, tape delay, the clatter and twang of spring reverb units. Dub's echoes create an illusion of space and add rhythmic complexity and density – in a music already lacking neither.

Sounds pan from one side of the mix to another. Dub's thick, languid, skittering strangeness, its disorienting and almost hallucinogenic – trippy – qualities, its alternation between familiarity and almost alienating strangeness: so many of its effects toy with our perception of space and time.

All of these studio transformations seem commonplace today, with the digital audio workstation software and a remix culture that is in part the *legacy* of dub. But in the 1970s dub was produced *quickly*, at the desk – dozens of mixes 'improvised on the spot', as Veal writes, on Friday evenings as weekend soundsystem operators gathered in wait.

The Jamaica diaspora brought dub to cities including Bristol and London, which hosted influential second-generation dub producers and soundsystem operators like Mad Professor and Jah Shaka.

Rob Smith, exposed to Bristol's Trinity Church where Jah Shaka played, remembered thinking '"Wow, my god, the room is actually shaking!" Then I realized it's my eyeballs in their sockets.' Later, he and Ray Mighty – as Smith & Mighty – would produce many of the groundbreaking singles that became known as trip-hop. 'Most people around us had exposure to reggae', recalled Ray Mighty, 'and were used to hearing music really loud … take the bass out, take the bass in, drop the beat in certain places … always some dub in there somewhere along the line'.

George Evelyn, known later as Nightmares on Wax, grew up in Leeds, in northern England. He heard jazz-funk and reggae and learned from soundsystems and the maximalism of dub engineer Scientist: 'bigger was better, bigger speakers bigger bass meant better, and that's how you were going to get your respect'.

Even a casual listen to a handful of the canonical dub records will reveal its full influence on 1990s' trip-hop: long basslines, languid tempos, a cavernous sense of space.[3] For example: King Tubby's *At the Controls*, or Augustus Pablo's *King Tubbys Meets Rockers Uptown* or *East of the River Nile*, or Lee Perry and The Upsetters' *Revolution Dub* (1975), Keith Hudson's *Pick a Dub*.

Or: King Tubby protege Scientist's *Scientist Rids the World of the Evil Curse of the Vampires* or *Scientist Meets the Space Invaders* (both released in 1981). Jah Shaka, *Commandments of Dub* (1982).

There was conscious and direct overlap: hear legendary roots vocalist (and future Massive Attack collaborator) Horace Andy's *In the Light Dub* (1977). And, perhaps obviously, the work of Mad Professor, who was to remix Massive Attack's second album into a full-length dub album in 1995's *No Protection* – his crisp, funky, sideways lilt in evidence as early as 1982's *Dub Me Crazy!!* and *Beyond the Realms of Dub*.

'It was unique at the time', he recalled of remixing *Protection*, 'because you didn't hear about pop bands doing dub albums'. The album is thoroughly transformed – ransacked, almost. But Mad Professor never lets the songs come apart, for – a dub engineer's craft – he is constantly coiling and defusing tension, *summoning* tension, somehow, into the original's deliberately cool and flat emotional affect. 'Sly' was the first song remixed: as 'Eternal Feedback' it bursts open in blistering, shining reverb before a series of stalled crescendos into smothering throb. 'Protection' was next: Tracey Thorn's voice no longer buoyed in the song's tilt but cast among cascades, rapids. Asked how he approached the project: 'Well, the same way. We strip it down and put it together. I mixed it how I would mix any other record.'

Dub's influence would resonate through the acts that would come out of Bristol, including Smith & Mighty, Massive Attack, Tricky, Portishead. Critics like Ian Tarr heard in Tricky's music the Rasta cosmology latent in dub: 'the same dammy palmed emotion: blunted paranoia, swollen into cosmic, millenarian dread. A sense that we're living through Armageddon Time; Babylon's last days'.

Tricky saw dub as 'an influence in that it isn't perfectionist. Dub, it's just bottom-end heavy with loads of noises, and it's not musically "correct"'. Dub's impulse to strip a track down to its elements and then cast them even further out in reverb would see it in alliance with hip-hop, ambient and industrial/noise music: a deconstructed, sparse, bass-first and oftentimes unsettling music. In the UK, this could be heard in the work of artists like Mick Harris of Scorn; in the very weird deconstructed hip-hop of DJ Vadim; musician/multi-disciplinarian artist Trevor Jackson's Skull project. And throughout the career of Kevin Martin, whose many identities include The Bug and Techno Animal.

Martin compiled a compilation series called *Macro Dub Infection*, taking a long and ranging tour of dub in all its mid-1990s' intersections with ambient, breakbeat, trip-hop, and drum & bass; and both volumes are a surprisingly soothing if thoroughgoing experience. Trip-hop acts are easily accommodated if in their most experimental form: Tricky's so-called ambient remix of 'Pumpkin', guttural bike rev under Alison Goldfrapp's gorgeous vocal, and Earthling's ten-minute 'Nothingness'.

In New York, some of hip-hop's formative elements can be credited to the Jamaican expatriates who brought with them dub's sensibilities and, perhaps, its toasting. The 'illbient' scene was a fractious coalition of dub, hip-hop and ambient, that ran in parallel to trip-hop. Skiz Fernando Jr. started the WordSound label, which put out strong compilations as *Crooklyn Dub Consortium*. He recorded as Spectre or The Ill Saint: 'what I called my genre was dub-hop'.

Gregor Asch – DJ Olive – told writer Laurent Fintoni:

> There was also an outer space, dark side of the moon element to dub that was really appealing. It was futuristic. A kind of sound where we were all foreigners but it made us all together.

In Europe, dub was a critical component in Berlin's early-1990s' underground techno scene. Mark Ernestus ran the Hard Wax record store, importing records from Chicago and Detroit's house and techno scenes. Ernestus and Moritz von Oswald formed Basic Channel, operating as label and artist in the early-to-mid 1990s. Their work combined dub and techno a in warm, synthetic mix of bass and decay (and skank) to induce a sense of pressure and trance. Multimedia artist Anna Piva remembered,

> a special place full of clubs and inner spaces. Beautiful, internal environments. When I first heard Mark and Moritz's music, what I heard was actually a very melancholic strain of sound. I wonder if it's something to do with, you know, with [Berlin's] history, that also comes across in the music. ... something to do with inner space as being a place of reflection and historical things.

Later, Ernestus and von Oswald formed Rhythm & Sound, collaborating with roots reggae singers. Their sound would be widely influential, including for their contemporaries Austrian trip-hop mainstays Peter Kruder and Richard Dorfmeister. Kruder & Dorfmeister became best known for their remix work, for artists as varied as Depeche Mode, Bone Thugs-N-Harmony, Bomb the Bass, and Madonna. Their months-long approach was the opposite of dub's spontaneity, but they were faithful to dub's unsparing methodology:

> The idea was always to deconstruct the original song as much as possible. Mostly, we just kept the vocals and composed a whole new song and feel around it.

Meanwhile, Stefan Betke, a former engineer at Basic Channel's Dubplates & Mastering facility, similarly released his *1*, *2* and *3* series within the influence of dub. He recorded as Pole, so named after a broken Waldorf 4-Pole filter that produced his characteristic glitchy sound. Pole's music has been widely influential – clearly audible in the work, say, of Canadian musician Scott Monteith (Deadbeat).

The 'glitch' aesthetic suggested something of the moment's transience. DJ M. Singe – Beth Coleman – was in Berlin in the early 1990s. She remembered:

> it was a real transitional time where people were so off-balance with the Wall coming down, and there were a lot of empty spaces that got filled up by underground scenes, club nights, installations. And it was massive; the music was incredible, and there was a feeling of: We can do whatever we think of, as long as we can figure out the technical way to pull it off. Nobody had any money; you just scrambled to put things together. … We did this kind of stuff where you just went and exploded all the time and didn't worry about this, that, or the other thing; and it was a time and a place where it was really good to be able to flow and not worry about the consequences.

Essential listening

- Massive Attack V Mad Professor, *No Protection* (Wild Bunch, 1995)
- Various, *Macro Dub Infection Volume One* (Virgin, 1995)
- Rhythm & Sound with Tikiman (Paul St. Hilaire), *Showcase* (Burial Mix, 1998)
- Various, *Crooklyn Dub Consortium: Certified Dope Vol. 2* (WordSound, 1996)
- The Bug, *Tapping the Conversation* (WordSound, 1997)

Also recommended

- Massive Attack V. Mad Professor, *Massive Attack V. Mad Professor Part II (Mezzanine Remix Tapes '98)* (Virgin, 2019)
- Rob Smith, *The Blue&Red Tapes Vol. 1* (RSD, 2020)
- Henry & Louis Meet Blue & Red, *Time Will Tell* (BSI, 2001)
- Kitachi, *A Strong Unit* (Dope On Plastic, 1996)
- Scorn, *Gyral* (Scorn, 1995)
- Scorn, *Logghi Barogghi* (Scorn, 1995)
- Techno Animal, *Re-Entry* (Virgin, 1995)
- Skull, *Snapz* (Output, 1999)
- Various, *Crooklyn Dub Consortium: Certified Dope Vol. 1* (WordSound, 1995)
- Deadbeat, *New World Observer* (~scape, 2005)

3 Lovers hip-hop

Bristol – blues parties – underground – The Wild Bunch – Lovers Rock – Smith & Mighty – Massive Attack

Rolling Stone suggested in 1996 that trip-hop's origins were to be found in 'the DJ-based Wild Bunch collective in the blue-collar port city of Bristol'.

The range of the Bristol's music scene has always defeated any notion of a 'Bristol sound' – even if its artists hadn't hated such media-imposed labels. 'Forget all that trip-hop bullshit', Andrew Vowles – Massive Attack's Mushroom – told *Mixmag* in 1998. 'When the Wild Bunch started, we called it lover's hip-hop.'

Still: Bristol did produce The Wild Bunch, and then Massive Attack, and Tricky; and Smith & Mighty; and Earthling; and (nearby) Portishead. And Bristol exemplifies many of the cities present in the biographies of other artists in this book – London, Paris, Marseilles, Antwerp, Brooklyn. These cities had been hubs in the Atlantic trade system and in European colonial empires. And as those empires retreated to their metropolitan cores by the 1980s these cities had become home to immigrant communities – from the Caribbean, from North Africa – whose music would meld in second generations with hip-hop's recombinative ethos and its surging social and cultural energy.

Bristol was a city of just under 400,000 in 1980, its aging wealth the product of its role as a hub in the slave trade. Bristol merchants in the eighteenth century were responsible for the abduction of perhaps half a million Africans in over two thousand Bristol-owned ships. The profits were still evident in the city's architecture – 'the palatial Clifton houses now converted into flats' wrote journalist Phil Johnson; and its legacy written in street names like Guinea Street and Jamaica Street and set in statues like that of Royal African Company member Edward Colston – that would not be cast down until the antiracist protests of 2020.

Bristol's St Paul's neighbourhood was home to many residents of Afro-Caribbean origin, particularly from Jamaica. Discrimination in the city had drawn national attention in the 1960s in the Bristol Bus Boycott. By 1980, it was rife in the dilapidated housing, the employment discrimination, the restive far-right National Front party, and the reviled police stop-and-search 'sus' law. In April 1980, the police raided St Paul's Black and White Café. Ray Mighty – later part of Smith & Mighty – told Ian Bourland in 2017:

> They were just messing with people so often and they caught it on the wrong day. They were raiding, and we decided to throw a brick at a van and caught four officers on their own and they were attacked and it spiralled from there. For eight hours, there was no law. The police got run out – they didn't have the equipment or the training. They didn't want to arrest anyone for the next 4-5 years. It was a no-go area for a while.

The St Paul's riot was part of a constellation of urban unrest – with protests and riots in the year ahead in London, Birmingham, Liverpool, Leeds – protesting a Monetarist-induced recession, unemployment, racism and aggressive policing.

Bristol's spaces for music and socializing were no less controlled than in other cities around the UK, where racial segregation was practised at the doors of clubs and bars every night of the week. 'The house parties were how you used to socialize', Trevor White remembered, 'because at the time the streets weren't safe in order to socialize to go to the pub. It was a no-no. You couldn't go to the pub. That was for English people.' Blues parties went back as far back as the 1950s and the first post-war Caribbean immigrants: held in people's houses (sometimes a modest door charge to cover costs), working class, a place of refuge and community as much as of terrific music on proper sound systems.

The sociologist Ken Pryce described entering a Bristol blues party of some 100–200 people – 'a dense, teeming, sweaty mass of humanity' – in his 1979 book *Endless Pressure*:

> Inside we remain motionless in the crowded passage, but trying all the same to push our way in. Blacks and whites are trying to escape to the nearest room where the dancing is taking place, but that room is just as packed. It is impossible, we cannot move backward or forward ... The two rooms packed with people opened into each other. In one of the rooms, there was only one sound-box or speaker. Here the atmosphere was lighter and the light brighter. There was more movement. The people were dancing rhythmically to the music. Pairs of people dance apart, thrusting their hands forward and backward as they do the reggae.

But the blues parties were treacherous refuge. In 1981, thirteen young Black Britons died in a fire at a teenage birthday party in London's New Cross area. Another victim died by suicide two years later. Despite National Front activity in the area, the police did little to pursue suspicions of arson. Instead they interrogated the survivors. The political establishment was indifferent. Amid the grief and the outrage and protest that followed, dub poet Linton Kwesi Johnson wrote 'New Craas Massakah': 'how di whole a black Britn did rack wid rage'.

For some, including DJ and sound system operator Norman Jay, the New Cross fire horribly materialized their fears about the blues dances. 'I can remember house parties where you could feel the floor bouncing up and down about four or five inches', he remembered. 'I can't understand why more didn't collapse'. They turned to other venues, pushing events even further underground. Those venues included the disused buildings in their thousands across London's deindustrializing landscape – much of it still unrebuilt in the post-war period and further depopulated by 'slum clearance' redevelopments and white flight. These spaces offered, as Bradley puts it, 'easier access and exits, and fewer nooks and crannies' and they would allow 'bigger, broader-based crowds'.

All of this would inform the music: precarious, intimate, improvisatory, political and – particularly in the case of the Wild Bunch – joyously eclectic. The Wild Bunch were Miles Johnson (DJ Milo), Nellee Hooper, Grant Marshall (Daddy G); and, later, Robert Del Naja (3D), Claude Williams (Willie Wee) and Andrew Vowles (Mushroom). And occasionally a very young Adrian Thaws – the Tricky Kid.

Tricky's cousin Michelle Porter recalled the scene in Bristol:

> it was lots of parties, and nights at warehouses, where we knew someone who was playing. It was always grotty places, none of the glamorous places – backstreet clubs, which attracted the people who came to hear music, dance and have a good time.

Johnson and Hooper already had some experience in the city's post-punk bands. Bristol had an eclectic post-punk scene including The Pop Group – with vocalist Mark Stewart – and Rip Rig + Panic; their music would bring together punk, dub, free jazz, and an agitprop avant-garde sensibility. Stewart told the BBC later:

> We wanted to mix in the stuff we were hearing in the clubs and streets and the sound systems and the blues dances of Bristol. Which was bassline. We were crashing and smashing and careering all the influences we heard on the streets of St Pauls and Bristol, in a punk manner, into what we were doing. Because we thought it wouldn't be punk to do something that was already happening.

The Wild Bunch made their reputation on their playlist, Johnson remembered: 'we were playing basically reggae, soul, jazz fusion and punk, new wave … I don't discriminate except where it comes to country music.' They were getting records no one else could, electro and underground Chicago house. Daddy G's day job was at Revolver, one of the city's best record stores. 'Other DJ crews used to complain because he'd stash away the good tunes so no one else could get them but us. Or sell them to kids who he knew weren't DJs.'

Those rival crews and sound systems included UD4, City Rockas, 2 Bad, FBI Crew, Three Stripe Posse (which included Smith & Mighty). Rivalry only intensified when hip-hop hit. 'People went mad for it', Rob Smith remembered, recalling a Kurtis Blow performance in Bristol around 1982. 'The very next day everybody was getting two decks wired together and cutting bits of newspaper out to make slipmats. It's like the whole city changed, literally overnight.'

Mark Stewart brought back from New York tapes recorded from radio stations like 98.7 KISS-FM and WBLS. And, as Ray Mighty remembered, Stewart 'started making these crazy electro-dub records … this punk-rocky indie sound with heavy dub effects and electronics'.

The Wild Bunch integrated hip-hop's two-turntables-and-a-microphone technique. In 1983 and 1984, they held an illegal party on the downs, the 400-acre park on the edge of the city. They threw a party at an abandoned warehouse, Red House, that brought out 2000. By 1985, they were playing St Paul's carnival, where DJ Krust remembered their astonishing stamina and reach:

> At Carnival they'd play a fifteen to twenty hour set … A system 15 feet high. You could hear them like 10 miles away. In the morning after one Carnival I walked home to my house on the other side of Bristol and when I got there I could still hear them.

And Johnson saw the legacy of the standoff back at the Black and White Café:

> Cops used to come along and see 500 to 700 people in the streets dancing and tried to shut us down. And nobody was having it really. They just shook their heads and left. I think the riots kind of gave us that freedom.

At the other extreme, The Dug Out club was destined to become famous among all the Bristol spaces. Rob Smith remembered that 'it was open every night and it was cheap. As everyone was on the dole, most people went there: punks, Rastas, soul boys, jazz people.' Matt Hall, later a BBC radio producer, remembered it as 'this really dank nasty club with this pinball table which the Wild Bunch basically colonized.

It was like a social club for them … No one else in town was going up to London to buy clothes or flying out to Japan for parties. They really were the coolest people in town.'

Ten years later, when Massive Attack, Tricky and Portishead were topping the charts and winning awards, the Dug Out club would be remembered as a place of radical cultural mixing. Reggae, hip-hop, punk, jazz, soul.[1] Robert Del Naja saw it as 'the only place you could mix':

> That's why the Dug Out was such a threat, that's why it got closed down …. the Dug Out brought the black people out of St Paul's into Clifton, and the traders – it was them who got it closed down – couldn't hack it at all. And nor could the Old Bill because it meant things weren't contained into one area and it freaked them out, it was anarchy you know?

What was to be found (and then lost) in trip-hop was not just the eclecticism of its influences. It was the spectacular range of its spaces – from the intimacy of a house party to the cavernous reach of an abandoned warehouse to the defiant exuberance of an outdoor rave and the communal inversion of carnival. The music contained mutiny, celebration, consolation.

And – refuge.

One more space: the dance. From the late 1970s, in blues parties and even sound systems, the smooth curves of Lovers Rock: lyrics draped in close harmony across the surface of songs; melodies in small intervals, few great dramatic leaps that might throw a couple out from one another's arms.

Lovers Rock was, in the words of British dub pioneer Dennis Bovell, 'this new hybrid of London-based reggae that was couple-dancing style, it wasn't hard, and it was all about love'. Bovell wrote – among many, many songs – 'Silly Games', a hit for Janet Kay in 1979. His musical partner John Kpiaye said, 'What we was trying to do was add more melodic content … A lot of vocal harmonies. And that had the effect of softening the music, making it much more laid back.'

Author Neferatiti Ife recalled

> it gave us a voice, as young Black people in this country. We were experiencing a lot of racism – racism from school, racism by being stopped by the police; and difficulties at home with our parents: our parents really didn't understand the system and what was going on. So Lovers Rock was like an escape for us.

Lovers Rock made stars of female vocalists including Janet Kay, Carroll Thompson and Louisa Mark. On their songs you can hear the vocal isolation; the smooth touch; and the contained, swaying emotional expression – all atop a bass-driven groove – which would infuse what became known as trip-hop.

When, a decade later, Massive Attack called their music 'Lovers hip-hop' it suggested both the expansive social and rhythmic energy of hip-hop *and* the warm intimacy of Lovers Rock.

Where did the breakthrough come from? One of Wild Bunch's few recordings featured, as a B-side, a version of the Bacharach/David song 'The Look of Love' – a song made famous by Dusty Springfield on the soundtrack of parodic 1967 Bond movie *Casino Royale*. The song was covered, like other Bacharach/David songs, by Dionne Warwick. The Wild Bunch version featured future Massive Attack singer Shara Nelson. Miles Johnson remembered,

At the time when I DJ'ed, I used to do a lot of blending. Getting Dennis Edwards' 'Don't Look Any Further' and running it with LL Cool J's 'I Need a Beat'. Stuff like that. I'd call it my rough with the smooth mix. And that's where the concept came from, of having a rough hip hop beat with a singer on it. So, it was this dub plate sort of vibe. Plus, I always loved that song, particularly the Dionne Warwick version.

Ray Mighty heard the potential in what Johnson was doing:

I thought yeah, this is hip, this is what I want to do … Tough, loud beats, the odd little sample and a vocal going on, slow, very rare groove with a dubby bass line in a stripped-back empty mix.

With Rob Smith, Mighty was Smith & Mighty, and they have as good a claim to have invented trip-hop as anyone – though, as producers and artists their careers have been restlessly cross-genre: dub, drum & bass, dubstep. Their debut gig, around 1986, was just 'a sequencer, some synths and a couple of drum machines'. Mighty remembered the impromptu collaboration that catalysed the formula for them:

There was a guy compèring the night, so there was a microphone onstage, and as we were playing our cover version of Erik Satie's 'Gymnopédie No. 1', Mark Stewart got up and shouted, 'This is fucking brilliant!' and pulled Tricky up there too. He started to chat over what we were doing, riding the sort of style you'd hear on early Massive Attack stuff – which instantly made us realize that we really needed vocals over what we were doing.

That performance became 'Stranger Than Love', released in 1987 under Mark Stewart's name with its drawling lyric ('somewhere there is a place for us') from Bernstein and Sondheim's *West Side Story*.

'Rob and Ray should get a lot more respect because they were the first people to mess about with Dionne Warwick things', said Stewart. The duo released covers of 'Walk On By' and 'Anyone Who Had a Heart' in 1988. Both songs are dated by 1980s' drum machine programming and synth textures, but vocalist Jackie Jackson is deft, tentative, right at the front of the mix. A sample from Dionne Warwick's original suddenly churns 'Walk On ...'. Both songs are faster than they sound. There's something still sparse, experimental about them.

Smith & Mighty spent years in creative dispute with label Polygram. For six years only their production for Carlton's lost classic *The Call is Strong* (1990) would be released. *Bass Is Maternal* finally came out in 1995. Despite its many highlights, to call it inconsistent and fragmentary is mostly to observe the point of their creative restlessness. That spirit would see them each collaborate and experiment across genre – including, as Jaz Klash, with LA producer and vocalist The Angel (60 Channels).

The Wild Bunch had already fractured by the time Island's 4th & Broadway imprint released two singles. Nellee Hooper would join London sound system/group Soul II Soul and become one of the decade's superproducers. Milo moved to Japan, where he recorded with hip-hop collective Major Force; then New York.

And, in 1988, Daddy G, 3D, Mushroom, and (sometimes) Tricky formed the core of Massive Attack. According to Miles Johnson, the name was coined by New York graffiti artist Brim: the 'underground massive'. Johnson said, 'I wanted to turn it into an acronym sort of thing so it would read as T.U.M.A. So, I added the word "attack" onto the end to make it work and it became The Underground Massive Attack. It got shortened from that'.

Their first single, 'Any Love', continued the 'rough with the smooth' approach. It was co produced by Smith & Mighty.

Massive Attack's debut album, *Blue Lines*, came out in 1991, the first masterpiece in what would be (retroactively) called trip-hop.

Massive Attack were first a collective, then a band, then a series of duos. Just as warmth runs through their music so does unrest and detente. 1994's *Protection* (with Nellee Hooper back for production) is an album of slow builds and elastic surfaces, of smothering comfort from vocalists Tracey Thorn, Nicolette – as well a lingering implication of danger.

If *Protection* is disquieting, 1998's *Mezzanine* is a squalling, throbbing, compound of claustrophobia and intimacy. A masterpiece, to be sure, though one usually treated as one of interiority and disaster, rather than a protest album. It was the album that finally fractured the trio – 'Are we a fucking punk band now?' Vowles is said to have shouted – and it has a force and malice in its punk mid-range, alongside the enveloping warmth of genre-making 'Teardrop' and 'Angel'. (Mad Professor's remixes meet *Mezzanine*'s ferrous disquiet with ferocious disarray.)

Mark Stewart recalled,

> If you hear *Blue Lines*, it's like walking around City Road, a little bit out of it after carnival or something, and just hearing all these things, just like washing over you. And they didn't polish it, they didn't – it's real, fucking real.

A Lovers hip-hop playlist

- The Wild Bunch 'The Look of Love' feat. Shara Nelson (1987)
- Mark Stewart + Maffia, 'This Is Stranger Than Love' (1987)

- Smith & Mighty, 'Walk On …' feat. Jackie Jackson (1988)
- Smith & Mighty, 'Anyone …' feat. Jackie Jackson (1988)
- Massive Attack, 'Any Love' feat. Carlton (1988)
- Bomb the Bass, 'Say a Little Prayer' feat. Maureen (1988)
- Fresh 4, 'Wishing on a Star' feat. Lizz. E (1989)
- Bomb the Bass, 'Winter in July' feat. Loretta Heywood (1991)
- Bomb the Bass, 'Love So True (Depth Charge Remix)' feat. Loretta Heywood (1991)
- Carlton, 'Love and Pain' (1991)
- Sade, 'Feel No Pain (Nellee Hooper Remix)' (1992)

Essential listening

- Massive Attack, *Blue Lines* (Wild Bunch, 1991)
- Massive Attack, *Protection* (Wild Bunch, 1994)
- Massive Attack, *Mezzanine* (Virgin, 1998)
- Smith & Mighty, *Bass Is Maternal* (More Rockers, 1995)
- Smith & Mighty, 'BBC Essential Mix' (mix, 1996)

Also recommended

- DJ Milo (mixed), *The Wild Bunch: Story of a Sound System* (Strut, 2002)
- Daddy G, *DJ-Kicks* (Studio !K7, 2004)
- Massive Attack, *Heligoland* (Virgin, 2010)
- Nicolette, *Now Is Early* (Shut Up And Dance Records, 1992)
- Neneh Cherry, *Homebrew* (Circa, 1992)
- Neneh Cherry, *Man* (Virgin, 1996)
- Carlton, *The Call Is Strong* (FFRR, 1990)

- Smith & Mighty, *Big World, Small World* (Studio !K7, 1999)
- Smith & Mighty, *Retrospective* (Studio !K7, 2004)
- Jaz Klash, Thru the Haze (Cup Of Tea, 1996)
- 60 Channels, *Tuned in Turned on* (World Domination, 1998)

4 Chill out

Raves – chillout rooms – ambient house – Howie B – Kruder and Dorfmeister – a succession of repetitive beats

Music was always threatening to unleash anarchy in the UK in the 1980s and early 1990s, no less than in punk's late-1970s ferment. Or so the headlines said. 'Drug Gangs Set Up Fortresses', screeched the *Evening Standard* in a front-page report of a 1993 raid on London's Rush FM pirate radio station, broadcasting from one of the six tower blocks in Hackney's notorious Nightingale Estate. One of the station's DJs – who would abseil into an abandoned twenty-first floor apartment from the roof – quipped, 'You can ask anyone in Hackney, right, how long they've been waiting to get something fixed in their house. But [the authorities are] quite willing to spend a lot of money to get a helicopter out to get two kids off a roof.'

Rush FM broadcast breakbeat hardcore, a fusion of house music's four-to-the-floor energy with ferociously accelerated hip-hop breakbeats. Hardcore had emerged amid one of the era's many moral panics: raves.

Raves were open-air soundsystem gatherings. Their locations were communicated via telephone answering services at the last minute to evade police interception. Ravegoers would meet at a designated a motorway junction, a service station. They would travel in convoy to locations that could be outlandish. Novelist Hari Kunzru recalled attending raves in 'A fallow field, a beach, an old World War II airstrip'. The raves were associated with a post-hippie drop-out itinerant counterculture movement, the New Age Travellers; but the largest would attract tens of thousands from across British society.

The music was – in the words of Tim Knight, who attended a rave on Chobham Common in 1992 – 'always unpredictable, underground and unrelenting in its hardcore attitude'. House, techno, dub. The music's development and its reception was fuelled by recreational drug use, particularly – but by no means exclusively (nothing about raves was exclusive, especially not the drugs) – the euphoria-enducing synthetic psychoactive MDMA: ecstasy.

For Kunzru the music was 'relentless, deliberately inhuman, the sound of a world accelerating towards some unimaginable, mechanized future'. There was the unabating four-to-the-floor and squelchy TB-303 bass synth of acid house. Acid house had been pioneered in the early 1980s by Black DJs in Chicago[1] and popularized in London clubs after DJs like Paul Oakenfold returned from Ibiza in 1987 with the blissed-up-with-ecstasy 'Balearic beat' sound.

The music needed a comedown just as did the drugs. Oakenfold was resident DJ at the Heaven club beneath London's Charing Cross station. He asked Alex Paterson and Jimmy Cauty to DJ at the White Room, the club's VIP bar, in the laid-back manner of the sessions that Cauty had previously held spontaneously at his basement studio. 'He didn't want anyone to dance in that room', recalled Paterson. Their sessions in the White Room (with Martin 'Youth' Glover) set the template for the 'chill out room' of clubs and raves in the years ahead. Matt Black, of proto-trip-hop duo Coldcut, remembered:

> Not everyone wanted to be in the main room, all the time, off their tits, bouncing up and down like a pneumatic drill. Some people wanted to chill out, they wanted to dance

more slowly, groove out, or they wanted to just sit down and talk with their friends. So that sort of music was being played in the chill out room.

Alex Paterson and Jimmy Cauty were also the original iteration of The Orb. Their 1989 debut single, 'A Huge Ever Growing Pulsating Brain That Rules from the Centre of the Ultraworld' – 'ambient house for the e generation' as the single's back cover sleeve put it – lapped together, across nineteen minutes, a Minnie Ripperton vocal refrain, nature sounds, curtains of synth figures, church bells, choral sounds and the very occasional turbulent breakbeat. *The Orb's Adventures beyond the Ultraworld*, their 1991 debut album, expanded on the ambient house formula. So did Cauty's other venture, The KLF, who released *Chill Out* in 1990: a combination of influences including Brian Eno-formulated ambient music, soundtrack and spoken word samples, Pink Floyd, Steve Reich, dub, hip-hop's sampling ethos (and the occasional breakbeat), textural synthesizer experimentation and environmental noise. (Strictly Kev, later of Ninja Tune house band DJ Food: 'They'd use whale noises, bird calls, thunderstorms, wave records, astronaut chatter'). *U.F.Orb* (1992) had a *much* more present dub influence, pumping and thickly bass-driven.

But all of this music could be incredibly gentle, thoughtful, wispy, bright in its melodicism; and it all somehow retained a woozy warmth. This would remain present in what became labelled as trip-hop through the 1990s, ranging from Fila Brazillia's many albums and remixes, to some of the impeccably dull sunnier downtempo of the 1990s' end.

Music for Babies (1994) was the debut album from Scottish producer Howard Bernstein (Howie B), who would produce for Tricky, Björk, U2 and even on a trip-hop album by former The Band songwriter/guitarist Robbie Robertson. (He would also start his own Pussyfoot label.) *Music for Babies* is calming, soothing, contemplative, drifting and also oddly unsettling, glitchy. It shifts through beatless ambient, dub, breakbeats, the plunging synths of 1980s sci-fi soundtracks.

Ambient house's influence could be heard also in the 'intelligent dance music' (another of the era's disparaging terms) of Future Sound of London, Autechre, µ-Ziq; and later music of delicate fracture like Boards of Canada's *Music Has the Right to Children* (1998).

The chill-out rooms themselves would play acts like Coldcut alongside ambient house – 'we were sort of the hip-hop equivalent of The Orb' recalled Matt Black.

Similarly at home was the music of Austrian duo Kruder & Dorfmeister. Peter Kruder and Richard Dorfmeister started working together in 1991, both with experience DJ'ing in Vienna, both in bands. Discovering hip-hop and sampling, they spend countless obsessive hours in their home studio – 'Original Bedroom Rockers', as they dryly referred to themselves on their debut EP *G-Stoned* (1993) – crafting stripped-down tracks that were unmistakably of hip-hop provenance, yet dubby in their bassy spaciousness, clubby in their glossy sheen.

Kruder & Dorfmeister's music had plenty of fellow travellers: the dub-lounge affectations of American duo Thievery Corporation, French tango/electronic group Gotan Project and German 'dubtronica' duo Boozoo Bajou.

Kruder and Dorfmeister went on to other projects: both Peace Orchestra and Tosca had strong first albums. The success of their remix work – collected on *The K&D Sessions* (1998) – overshadowed the absence of a full-length album under their own name. It's now almost impossible to hear their music except through the dull music it inspired. Even they agreed that as the decade progressed 'the so called downbeat/triphop style was more and more watered down by semi-cool compilations overusing the word chill out'. The material planned for their debut came out more than two decades later. Reflecting on the reception of their music in the 1990s, they remarked, 'It was original when we made it'.

Chill-out rooms were very literally an opportunity for clubbers and ravers to restore their body temperature. And though the music had a suffusing light touch – its unremitting rhythm not always audible but ever-present – it nonetheless imbued a sense of collective (if pharmacologically induced) unconsciousness.

That collectivity was perhaps the most disruptive aspect of rave culture, appearing in an era in which Margaret Thatcher had suggested, in 1987, 'there is no such thing as society' and the Conservatives endlessly extolled the office worker as the only irreducible social entity of worth. Kunzru felt 'a sort of ecstatic fantasy of community, a zone where we were networked with each other, rather than with the office switchboard'. Tim Knight was one of 'so many people who once thought that they were students, or hairdressers, or bank clerks, instead became ravers, with reality an unfortunate necessity'. To some the raves suggested a defiance of the era's racial stratifications: 'What really strikes me is how multi-racial they were', said DJ and music producer Andrew Weatherall.

The establishment panicked. The 1980s conservative consensus had seen out the urban racial unrest of the early 1980s and smashed the labour movement in the 1984–1985 miners' strike. Now, even as the 1989 fall of the Berlin

Wall had seemed to consolidate the triumph of Western market capitalism, tens of thousands of young people were celebrating in huge numbers the dissolution of their own consciousness. Anthony Burgess decried 'the megacrowd, reducing the individual intelligence to that of an amoeba'. This was happening on the literal ground zero of capitalism where, centuries earlier, enclosure to private property had dispossessed people to an itinerant urban poor that could be made subject to unfree labour conditions.

The Conservative government responded with a traditional vortex of fear, categorization, and policing. MP Michael Spicer described the 1992 week-long Castlemorton festival as an 'invasion':

> new age travellers, ravers and drugs racketeers arrived at a strength of two motorised army divisions, complete with several massed bands and, above all, a highly sophisticated command and signals system.

Spicer warned of 'vigilante groups' and 'anarchy and chaos'; MPs debated redefining the 'traditional nomadic habit type gipsies' to strip legal shelter from 'a bunch of unwashed, benefit-grabbing, socialist anarchists who deserve a good slap and a wash'. Among the debates' most absurd efforts to 'catch' some events yet permit others, the House of Lords debated the meaning of 'night'.

The resulting legislation – the Criminal Justice and Public Order Act 1994 – gave police stop and search powers within five miles of a rave; the power to confiscate and disable (destroy) private property including soundsystem equipment; and, notoriously, it defined a 'rave' as an open air gathering with 'sounds wholly or predominantly characterised by the emission of a succession of repetitive beats'.

The legislation passed – with the acquiescence of a young Tony Blair, then shadow home secretary. There was protest and activism; the occupation of disused buildings. But police set up exclusion zones and blocked motorway exits and they seized and destroyed sound systems. It was over. Something of the rave scene survived into continental Europe – and, in a thoroughly cleaned up version, in the festival circuit. But for dance music the end of raves precipitated the era of giant commercial clubs (and the superstar DJ), so often in repurposed warehouses and industrial buildings – making the music, in its own way, a gateway to gentrification.

Moreover, the music establishment would throughout the years ahead persistently whitewash the musics that arose from breakbeat hardcore. This was consistent with the same deprecation of the Black (and queer) subcultures that had created acid house in the first place. As we'll see, trip-hop – at least in its relationship to hip-hop and dub – felt, at times, like a similar act of erasure.

And where, for the Tories, music so often represented anarchy, for Tony Blair's New Labour government in the back half of the 1990s, music was a matter of national pride – a cultural export to advertise the virtues of a purportedly progressive, multicultural nation without talking much about the history that created it or the conditions that informed it.

Music's accessorization by the establishment was something in which trip-hop was to become implicated, in part by gradually substituting an ahistorical nostalgia for an engagement with the dub, Lovers Rock, breakbeat culture and punk from which it drew. In this it was aided, in part, by the kind of pastoralism suggested by all those nature sounds – and imagery, as on the cover of *Chill Out*, depicting the rural scenes in which ravers would come down to ambient house.

Essential listening

- The KLF, *Chill Out* (1990) (re-edited as *Come Down Dawn* by The Justified Ancients of Mu Mu, 2021)
- The Orb, *The Orb's Adventures beyond the Ultraworld* (Big Life, 1991)
- Howie B, *Music for Babies* (Polydor, 1996)
- Kruder & Dorfmeister, *G-Stoned* EP (G-Stone, 1993)
- Kruder & Dorfmeister, *The K&D Sessions* (Studio !K7, G-Stone, 1998)
- Kruder & Dorfmeister, *1995* (G-Stone, 2020)
- Tosca, *Opera* (G-Stone, 1997)
- Peace Orchestra, *Peace Orchestra* (G-Stone, 1999)
- Boards of Canada, *Music Has the Right to Children* (Warp, 1998)

Also recommended

- Fila Brazilia, *Brazilification: Remixes 95–99* (Kudos, 1999)
- Rockers Hi-Fi, *Mish Mash* (Different Drummer, 1996)
- Freak Power, *In Dub: The Fried Funk Food EP* (Island, 1994)
- Thievery Corporation, *Sounds from the Thievery Hi-Fi* (Eighteenth Street Lounge, 1996)
- Gotan Project, *La Revancha Del Tango* (¡Ya Basta!, 2001)
- Tosca, *Suzuki* (G-Stone, 2000)

5   Cut up

Hip-hop collage – Major Force – Coldcut – Ninja Tune –
Nightmares on Wax

When *Smokers Delight*, the second album by Nightmares on
Wax (George Evelyn), came out in 1995, he was outraged by
the 'trip-hop' label. For there had *already* been a rich tradition of
'instrumental hip-hop tracks made up of samples ... They were
galactic-sounding and were never perceived as "trip hop."'

In the mid-1970s, DJ Kool Herc had pioneered the
'Merry-Go-Round' technique: the same record spinning
on two turntables, so that an instrumental break could be
endlessly repeated to keep the dancefloor alive. 'Under the
counter' compilations (with titles like *Super Disco Brake's* [sic.]
and *Ultimate Breaks & Beats*) of classic funk and jazz-funk
instrumental tracks soon appeared for DJs (and producers)
to shortcut the abruptly expensive collecting of records
suddenly in demand.

Soon, DJs were using multiple turntables or cassette decks
to combine components from *multiple* records. Examples
included Grandmaster Flash's three-turntables performance 'The
Adventures of Grandmaster Flash on the Wheels of Steel' (1981);
and Afrika Islam's 1980 'Fusion Beats Vol. 2' – put together with 'a
pause button in my bedroom! I paused that on a cassette tape.'

Afrika Islam remembered, 'we were doing these mash-ups
throughout hip-hop history. ["Fusion Beats"] is one that just
happened to have made it to becoming vinyl. All the rest were
done on acetates or they were being played directly from

cassette. We were always using a beatbox in the club, we were always splicing together beats so people could rap off of it.'

Other essential records in the cut-up tradition included Double Dee and Steinski's 'Lessons' series. Doug DiFranco and Steve Stein were two white hip-hop enthusiasts well into their careers as a sound engineer and advertising copywriter; their 'The Payoff Mix' (1983) was an entry in a remix competition for Tommy Boy records. Assembled through hours of cutting and pasting tape, the track collated in five minutes a blistering mix of contemporary hip-hop, classic break sources ('Apache', James Brown's 'Soul Power'), New Wave and synth pop (Culture Club, Yazoo), Herbie Hancock, Indeep, Little Richard, The Supremes, vintage movie dialogue.

'Lesson 2 (James Brown Mix)' and 'Lesson 3 (History of Hip Hop Mix)' followed in 1984 and 1985, respectively. Never officially released – there were innumerable copyright issues – but widely available as bootlegs and white labels, these records are flashy, brisk, disjunctive, kinetic, almost by definition ironic in their juxtapositions and overlaps; as much exhibitions as records, perhaps. Hip-hop's instrumental cut-up records, at their best, represented feats of DIY technology and musicality, theoretically available to anyone with a record collection and a couple of turntables – or a cassette deck with a pause button. Creating a 'Lessons'-style mix was to become a calling card for virtuoso DJ-producers well into the 1990s, including Dan the Automator, DJ Shadow, Cut Chemist and Nu-Mark. And in the years ahead, this hip-hop instrumental tradition continued in 12-inches, B-sides, whitelabels.

In 1985, John Oswald coined the term 'Plunderphonics' in an essay – its subtitle 'Audio Piracy as a Compositional Prerogative' – very pleased with its suggestion that divisions between listener and producer were being eroded by technology, with commercial and legal structures (like copyright) unable to keep up. Hip-hop seemed to some a popular corroboration of postmodern theory's fascination with bricolage and pastiche; and Oswald's essay exhibited postmodernism's slippery optimism, the suggestion that a kind of sabotage might be done to hierarchies simply by trading things out of context. That notion would become as familiar, in the decades ahead, as its disappointments. Still, in Oswald's observation that 'Now that keyboardists are getting instruments with the button for this appropriation built in, they're going to push it' was a premonition of hip-hop's unstoppable trajectory beyond the United States. To take just one example, in Mantronix's 'King of the Beats' (1988), amid six minutes of breakbeat collage, producer Kurtis Mantronik detonated a genre-inspiring manipulation of the drum break from The Winstons' 'Amen, Brother'.

It's easy to forget how experimental this music was; but rediscovering that sense of wonder is helpful to understand how records like this were to become so influential. For the last minute or so of the 12" release, the beat suddenly drops to a slower tempo and becomes more abstract: sampling artefacts, lo-fi, spinning on its own inertia. Mantronik remembered playing it for Capitol Records, who had just paid a significant advance to sign Mantronix from Sleeping Bag.

> I knew there were a lot of hip-hop heads there so I always had this thing like, 'I got to do some beats, I got to mess them up'. 'King of the Beats' was the introduction. The siren came on and then some people were like, 'Ah,' but mostly they were just sitting there. I don't know if they were in awe, or if they were just like, 'What the hell is this?' That moment was when I started to slowly leave the music business.

Japanese musician Toshio Nakanishi (Toshi, Tycoon To$h), graphic designer, owner of Tokyo club Pithecanthropus Erectus, saw Afrika Bambaataa while touring New York with Melon, and found – alongside *Blade Runner* and the 1950s American literary movement known as the Beat Generation – influences for a pivotal role in Japanese hip-hop.

Back in Japan, Toshi founded Major Force in 1987 with a collective that included Masayuki Kudo and Gota Yashiki. The label's first release was from Tiny Panx, whose 'Last Orgy' is clearly in the tradition of old school hip-hop and 'Lessons'. So is Hiroshi Fujirwara and Kudo's collaboration with the Wild Bunch's DJ Milo, 'The Original Art-Form' – 'one of the greatest collage records of its time' according to Mo'Wax founder James Lavelle.

Major Force was an aesthetic, a lifestyle as much as a label, with stunning graphic design and even streetwear. With collaborations with American hip-hop crews and British sound system culture, their influence stretched well beyond Japan – including inspiring Lavelle.

Toshi and Kudo relocated to London in the early 1990s and found

> a real psychedelic atmosphere, like in the '60s ... It wasn't the acid of ecstasy like the Manchester bands, it was the real psychedelic acid. Due to this, we tried to make psychedelic hip hop. In terms of records, England is the origin of psychedelic rock, and so there were lots to be dug out. Though, there, it would be called trip-hop.

The music they would put together in London, as Major Force West, was exactly as that would suggest: draggy, psychedelic in an Age-of-Aquarius type way, goopy, languid.

Also in London were Matt Black and Jonathan More. 'We were these white guys just really fucking totally in love with Black music', recalled Black of his formative years. In 1986, he and More, as Coldcut, self-released 500 copies of 'Say Kids (What Time Is It?)', using a soldering iron to obscure the pressing plant details and prevent copyright disputes being tracked back to them. 'Say Kids' was a dizzying, high-energy melange of classic hip-hop breaks, hip-hop quotes, funk, showers of movie soundtracks and dialogue – and the energy and irreverence of acid house which, like many British DJs at the time, Black brought back from a stint DJ'ing in Spain. And like the records to follow – 'Beats + Pieces'; the 'journey into sound' seven-minute remix of Eric B's & Rakim's 'Paid in Full' – all of it was informed by the tradition of the 'Lessons' series.

But they soon found themselves in the 'sausage machine swamp of the music business'. Label/management Big Life pushed a commercial template; and their debut album *What's That Noise* (1989) was the resulting pop-housey turnablist collage with occasional vocal.

Coldcut's first releases coincided with a brief surge in UK popularity of sample-based acid-house-and-hip-hop mashups. M|A|R|R|S, a one-off combination of Colourbox and proto-shoegaze/proto-dreampop/pre-post-rock duo A.R. Kane, scored a massive UK and Euro hit with 'Pump Up the Volume' (1987). So too did S'Express with 'Theme from S-Express' (1988) ('enjoy this trip', advised the cover art). Tim Simenon's Bomb the Bass broke out with *Dragnet*-sampling samplefest 'Beat Dis' (1987). And Jonathan Saul Kane, recording as Depth Charge, released a series of singles and EPs starting with 1989's 'Bounty Killer'.

Yearning to return to experimental, instrumental hip-hop, Coldcut resolved to start their own label, but they couldn't record under their own name until major label contracts elapsed. Their label's name was inspired by a trip to Japan: Ninja Tune – for ninjas 'were all about artifice and hidden identity'.

Among their new aliases for Ninja Tune was DJ Food, with five volumes of *Jazz Brakes* loop-based instrumental hip-hop compositions released between 1990 and 1995, intended to fill out a working DJ's crate. (The spelling was suggested by those *Super Disco Brake's* collections.)

1993's *Philosophy* was released while they were still under major label contract. It contained 'Eine Kleine Hed Musik' with its churning Grant Green break and 'Signs' – early trip-hop classics. (Also essential is the Mixmaster Morris ambient remix of 'Autumn Leaves'.) But the album was pop radio-friendly acid jazz, fronted by vocalist Janis Alexander, sparingly topped with breakbeats.

It was in stark contrast to the 'experimental, instrumental, dubby hip-hop', they were meanwhile putting out on Ninja Tune – most of which wasn't selling terribly well. The *Jazz Brakes* 'were keeping the whole thing afloat, really', recalled label manager Peter Quicke. 'We realized we should concentrate on that jazzy, hip-hop instrumental sound.'

More British hip-hop enthusiasts would come to Ninja Tune. DJ Food would presently expand to include Patrick Carpenter (PC) and Kevin Foakes (Strictly Kev).[1] *A Recipe for Disaster* (1995) extended the goofy, unstable beat collage experimentation of *Jazz Brakes* with a saturated, moody, instrumental hip-hop. And 2000's *Kaleidoscope* would have a terrific middle section, including their masterpiece 'The Crow', a limber, elegiac sweep of a song that builds through its rumbling bass melody to a cinematic crescendo.

Jake Wherry and Ollie Teeba would sign as Herbaliser, self-consciously imitating Coldcut down to the 'old Hollywood samples over the top'. There is a DJ's sense of gravity in their music: there's always something orbiting the core of a song, there under all the unflagging samples. 'Another Mother', from *Blow Your Headphones* (1997), is a clear statement of the mid-1990s Ninja Tune sound: drifting, dark, spacious, a loping unresolved bass line; squalling, drifting samples, a reverby tendril of a guitar line, slightly decayed drum sounds. A bit mysterious, but let's not exaggerate. Accessible.

Ninja would hold this approach throughout the decade, signing for example – Canadian Kid Koala, who can make a turntable breathe, hum, cry, sigh, sound like a harmonica, sound like a small dog howling when an ambulance goes by, etc. Kid Koala's music is genuinely funny where many latter-day 'Lessons' beat collages are exhausting demonstrations of technique; yet there is also a darker edge in his music: a melancholic, ever-present melodicism; something weird, keening and mournful.

Nightmares on Wax were originally George Evelyn and Kevin Harper They came out of Northern England's post rave 'bleep' techno sub-genre. Their debut, *A Word of Science*, was free-ranging, uptempo early 1990s' British electronic dance music. Its opener, 'Nights Interlude', is a classic: a summery, hazy theme built around a low-pass sample of Quincy Jones' 'Summer in the City'. Evelyn would return to it in openers for his following albums, tracking the decade's progress as the music went from dusty samples to taut jazz-funk to something rumbling, electronic, symphonic.

Evelyn was on his own for *Smokers Delight*. It combined 'all the things that turned me on', Evelyn recalled: 'reggae, soul … the dub influences on there, and the lovers rock soulful influence'. But there was one thing pulling it all together. The liner notes couldn't be clearer: 'the media try to fool the young B-Boys "n" Girls with trendy names such as "TRIP HOP" but at the end of the day "HIP HOP" is "HIP HOP"'.

Essential listening

- Various, *Major Force (The Original Art-Form)* (Mo'Wax, 1997)
- Major Force West, *93–97* (Mo'Wax, 1999)
- Various, *Cold Krush Cuts* (Ninja Tune, 1996)
- Coldcut, *Journeys by DJ: 70 Minutes of Madness* (Music Unites, 1995)
- DJ Food, *A Recipe for Disaster* (Ninja Tune, 1995)
- DJ Food, *Kaleidoscope* (Ninja Tune, 2000)
- The Herbaliser, *Remedies* (Ninja Tune, 1995)
- The Herbaliser, *Blow Your Headphones* (Ninja Tune, 1997)
- Nightmares on Wax, *Smokers Delight* (Warp, 1995)
- Kid Koala, *Carpal Tunnel Syndrome* (Ninja Tune, 2000)

Also recommended

- Coldcut, *Let Us Play* (Ninja Tune, 1997)
- Depth Charge, *Nine Deadly Venoms* (Vinyl Solution, 1994)
- Depth Charge, *Legend of the Golden Snake* EP (D.C., 1995)
- Various, *Flexistentialism* (Ninja Tune, 1996)
- DJ Food, *Refried Food* (Ninja Tune, 1996)
- A.P.E., *Striplight* (Dorado, 1995)
- Beat Demons, *Ghetto Jazz* (New Breed, 1995)

- Emapea, *Seeds, Roots & Fruits* (Cold Busted, 2016)
- Nightmares on Wax, *A Word of Science (The 1st & Final Chapter)* (Warp, 1991)
- Nightmares on Wax, *Carboot Soul* (Warp, 1999)
- Tim 'Love' Lee, *Confessions of A Selector* (Tummy Touch, 1997)
- Kid Koala, *Scratchcratchratchatch* EP (Ninja Tune, 1996)
- Kid Koala, *Space Cadet (Original Still Picture Score)* (Ninja Tune, 2011)
- Kid Koala, *12 Bit Blues* (Ninja Tune, 2011)

6 Contemplating jazz

Acid jazz – Sade – Mo' Wax – cool — Attica Blues

Trip-hop was named out of acid jazz; acid jazz was named out of a joke. DJs Gilles Peterson and Chris Bangs were following a rapturous set by acid house DJ Paul Oakenfold one night in 1987 at the Brentford Arts Centre.

> Gilles was spinning this old Sabu Martinez track[1] and there was a giant screen behind us showing psychedelic photos, graffiti art and text. So there's this heavy Latin track spinning and the screen keeps flashing up 'ACID … ACID' behind us in giant letters and we thought it was well funny. I grabbed the mike and shouted 'Fuck Acid House – This Is Acid Jazz!'

Acid house; acid jazz; acid hip-hop: trip-hop. The term acknowledged the trance-link state in which the music (and the Ecstasy) rinsed a crowd.

On Sunday afternoons from 1986 to 1991, the Dingwalls club in north London's Camden area hosted DJs Gilles Peterson and Patrick Forge. Their 'Talkin' Loud And Sayin' Something' sessions a sustained conversation with the crowd, including those from the underground jazz dance scene. Find videos on YouTube of dance groups like IDJ and you will see a style of dance that is florid in its coalitions of movement, is acrobatic, intricate, virtuosic and joyous; the dancers themselves young, Black, mostly male, from working-class communities across the UK; moves drawn from jazz, Hollywood musicals, martial arts films, ska, tap, ballet; a relentlessly competitive celebration of Black excellence, innovation and heritage.

The dancers pushed DJs like Peterson and Forge to higher levels of tempo and rhythmic complexity. Mo' Wax founder James Lavelle, who for years DJ'd alongside Peterson, recalled the reaction when dropping a record like Airto's 'Samba de Flora':

> You just had to bring the joy back in the mix ... when you dropped it in the mix the place would explode. It was just this incredible energy. Suddenly all these jazz dancers would be just doing the most incredible stuff. You'd have this just joyous explosion of people dancing. It was really cool when you'd take it on a really dark tangent and then come back around and come in with some record like this.

Acid jazz – and so part of trip-hop – came from the rare groove London DJ culture that which played out through the 1980s across the city's pirate radio and warehouse parties and underground clubs long after London's closing times. DJs like Norman Jay brought American soul and funk to audiences, many of whom had never heard it before. ('Most of the black kids already knew those records,' remembered Jay; 'it was white England discovering those records.')

Soundsystem audiences were changing too. Jazzie B, who founded North London soundsystem Jah Rico with teenage friend Daddae, remembered 'there was young white boys and girls from working-class backgrounds, who were far more integrated'. Jah Rico became Soul II Soul, turning their decks around to face the crowd so 'we could all be part of the same experience'; adding soul and funk; and developing a complete aesthetic identity in the 'Funki Dred' philosophy and look, the club flyers, comic books and clothing sold at Soul II Soul shops and market stalls. In 1986, they began their legendary run at the Africa Centre in Covent Garden, introducing live elements and eventually become a chart-topping band (including Lovers Rock singer Caron Wheeler and a post-Wild Bunch Nellee Hooper), their debut album *Club Classics Volume 1* (1989) a global hit.

The popularity of rare groove brought old-school American funk talent to London, including the legendary JBs on valedictory tours in 1987 and 1988. On that tour was James Brown's goddaughter Carleen Anderson, who backstage founded Young Disciples with Marco Nelson and Femi Williams. Their 1991 one-and-done album *Road to Freedom* should sit alongside Soul II Soul's *Club Classics Vol. One* and Massive Attack's *Blue Lines* as key genre-crossing albums of the time: soul, acid jazz, hip-hop.

Carleen Anderson's cousin Jhelisa Anderson was in London too, as part of Soul Family Sensation, whose 1991 album *New Wave* had just too much remnant 1980s sentimentalism amid its synths and drum machine patterns to last. But solo debut *Galactica Rush* (1994) yielded a classic in 'Friendly Pressure'. And *Galactica Dub*, a limited-edition tour EP, scraped away the smooth jazz and left Jhelisa's timing and soulful inflection against hauntingly abstract dub and electronic arrangements.

Unsurprisingly, given its rare groove origins, many of the acid jazz records – The Brand New Heavies, Galliano, Corduroy, Jamiroquai – had a danceable jazz-funk sound. In these and records by D'Influence and Omar it's easy to hear a kind of British alternative path to what became neo-soul.

Acid jazz's vocal side had a tendency to lounge, something that would follow into accomplished trip-hop acts like Morcheeba and Smoke City. It carried the enormous influence of Sade, whose 1984 single 'Smooth Operator', from *Diamond*

Life, had established a smooth, jazz-inflected soul pop that would have commercial appeal through the 1980s. Sade Adu's distinctive croon set against swaying rhythmic background – Sade can swing almost any arrangement – was to be widely influential. And one of the best albums to highlight that influence was Esthero's *Breath From Another* (1998) – not from London but Canadian singer/songwriter Jenny-Bea Englishman and Twin Cities producer Doc McKinney. The album has enough polish to hide how abstract McKinney's hip-hop– (and New Jack Swing–) infused production can be; Englishman's vocal inflections and timing find suspense even where the songs seem conventional.

The London scene in those years was eclectic, energetic and open-minded. Peter Adarkwah, who went on to co-found the Barely Breaking Even label, remembered:

> It was a time in London where there was just this constant stream of music, music blaring out of every car. ... I listened to Gilles Peterson and Patrick Forge and learnt about Brazilian music and folk ... We called '88' in London the second summer of love. The house and acid thing had started, rare groove was in overdrive and it was a classic era of hip hop with EPMD, Public Enemy and A Tribe Called Quest in their prime. ... Then you had the classic house of Marshall Jefferson, Todd Terry and deeper techier acid stuff. James Brown, Maceo Parker ... Donald Blackman's 'Blues for Warrior Spirit' all over the dance floor.

James Lavelle had been a DJ at 14 in his hometown Oxford, struck by American hip-hop and influenced by the

1980s' British sound system culture coming out of Bristol: Smith & Mighty, The Wild Bunch. He was already building a massive record collection. His sound system night in Oxford was named Mo' Wax Please – 'you'd play James Brown next to Nightmares on Wax next to EPMD and it was really exciting' – started with friends including Tim Goldsworthy. As a teenager he was working in London's Bluebird Records, in Paddington, and then Honest Jon's on Portobello Road.

> These types of independent record shops were like social meccas for this underground culture … As well as hearing all the new records, you would see all the real heads from the clubs, see what people were wearing, how they were speaking. Every part of it was an education.

Peter Bradshaw, founder of the London jazz dance scene magazine *Straight No Chaser,* remembered Lavelle 'totally stoked on Star Wars, kung fu, New York subway graffiti, hip-hop and all things Japanese'. He agreed to Lavelle's pitch for a column, 'Mo' Wax Please', which first ran in the Spring 1992 issue.

In his first few columns, Lavelle covered releases not just from the London scene, but also the vibrant acid jazz scenes of France and Italy and Brazil. And Japan: acts represented by Major Force; DJ Krush's collaborations with singer Monday Michiru; early releases from United Future Organization (for whom Lavelle and Goldsworthy did a nine-minute 'Men from U.N.K.L.E.' remix). And hip-hop: Cypress Hill, Common, Digable Planets, The Pharcyde, Pete Rock.

He also teased early releases on his own label. Mo' Wax. One of managers at Honest Jon's lent him £1,000 to fly to New York and sign acid jazz band Repercussions for 'Promise'. A pressing of 1,000 copies came out in 1992 as MW001.

'Promise' was, according to the liner notes, 'an immaculate groove of soul spiced with funk, jazz, salsa and hip hop'. True, Mo' Wax's early releases decidedly favoured acid jazz: Simon Richmond's Palm Skin Productions and Bubbatunes; Marden Hill; Bristol-based The Federation; an appallingly named *Jazz Hip Jap Project* compiling tracks from Japan's acid jazz scene. But Lavelle saw Mo' Wax pressing beyond the acid jazz sound. 'I didn't want that whole 'Cinzano Bianco' flavour, I wanted something just a little more rough. … Mo' Wax, it's younger, a bit more out of order'.

That edge would mostly be provided by hip-hop, which would inform the maximalist scene-defining ambitions that Lavelle had for the label – inspired by Major Force and the Wild Bunch and Soul II Soul. Yet, for the brief years that Mo' Wax was a vibrant and active label, it would remain true to the 'progressive electro' term that Lavelle used to describe DJ Krush's early remix track 'Just Wanna Touch Her — Stoned Jazz Mix'.[2] Lavelle saw Mo' Wax addressing the ways in which British music had fractured into different camps. It would remain a big tent label, one that could easily accommodate a release like 1997's *Big Soup* from Luke Vibert, whose music spans an endless stream of identities across an endless stream of genres.[3] Pablo Clements, a later collaborator, put it this way: 'Mo' Wax was the label that really spoke to everyone, like: techno, drum & bass, hip-hop, and acid jazz. Mo' Wax was the label that brought them people back together. It was doing what hadn't been done'.

Listening back now it is hard to escape the feeling that some of this music's engagement with jazz was mostly textural – whether the acid jazz flavours of early Mo' Wax or the direction that Ninja Tune found with the *Jazz Brakes* series. Ninja Tune's mid-1990s' roster included busy, bassy jazz-funk freneticism from Up, Bustle & Out and London Funk Allstars. And the snack-sized collisions of acid jazz and instrumental hip-hop from James Braddell's 9 Lazy 9 (with Keir Fraser) and Funki Porcini. These projects were self-consciously humorous, to be sure. But at times it sounded as if you had dropped a packet of mentos into a lava lamp.

A superficial and retro engagement with jazz was certainly apparent in trip-hop's early visual style. Mo' Wax's early visual direction was set by *Straight No Chaser* art director Swifty, whose influences included 'Saul Bass title sequences to Reid Miles' Blue Note record covers, Charles Eames furniture to Brutalist architecture'. When The Young Disciples asked for a design based on jazz saxophonist Joe Henderson's 1966 album *Mode for Joe:*

> I thought, since hip-hop was sampling old music and turning it into something new, I'm going to do the same with the visuals. That was where it all started for me, the whole appropriation, visual remixing thing.

A compilation series on 4th & Broadway named *The Rebirth of Cool*, curated by Patrick Forge, collected many of the records from the boundaries of jazz, hip-hop, acid jazz and their emergent combinations with electronic music. Swifty's design for the series paid homage to the legendary Blue Note jazz label: designer Reid Miles's spare, modernist sensibility in uninterrupted colours, blues, indigos, sans-serif typefaces and inset ovals; moody black & white photography. Swifty put together the Mo' Wax logo 'in about 20 minutes'. His designs for Mo' Wax's earliest releases, produced on a minimal budget, used a vertical 'obi strip' concept suggested by the Japanese Blue Note reissues that Lavelle and Swifty would see come through the magazine's office.

And not just them. Portishead's debut album, *Dummy* (1994), and its triptych of singles, 'Sour Times', 'Numb' and 'Glory Box' all clearly reference a Blue Note aesthetic. Monochrome stills of Beth Gibbons, taken from the band's promotional short film, suggested a noir movie which is also a science fiction movie which is also a medical abduction movie which is also a femme fatale revenge movie which is also a jazz album.

All of this was avowedly cool. 'Cool', said the liner notes from *The Rebirth of the Cool Phive*, 'can mean fascism; but here "cool" means freedom. Real cool is when nothing is uncool. When everything is possible. When you start to create without any preconceived notions of what you're suppose to do.'

Of course, the series was named in reference to the early 1950s *Birth of the Cool* sessions, which ushered in a period of jazz in which the harmonic innovations and melodic superabundance of 1940s bebop (a self-consciously Black response to the appropriations of earlier forms of jazz), were chilled in a soggy West Coast melancholy, cloaked it in forms of European classical music, and celebrated in white musicians like Gerry Mulligan, Chet Baker, and Dave Brubeck.[4] Jazz critic Frank Kofsky argued that cool was 'an attempt by white musicians to divorce jazz from its historical black moorings and transform it into a music with which they felt more at ease'.

And in hindsight, it's hard not to make the uncomfortable suggestion that trip-hop bears the same relationship to its sources, particularly hip-hop, as did cool jazz to its own. It's not as if the *sound* of trip-hop was the sound of cool jazz, notwithstanding the Dave Brubeck sample that burps into the start of 'Rose Rouge' on St Germain's jazz/lounge mainstay

Tourist (2000). Where trip-hop sampled jazz, it was mostly the same bluesy, soulful, and self-consciously Black hard bop that was sampled into hip-hop. Yet trip-hop could have something of cool's sonic aspect: almost *designed* to be mood music, bar music, lounge music; politically inert, a tonal range rarely ventured from personal isolation or glossy, supine texture. Music to look cool to.

For these were the years, into the 1990s, in which as writer David H. Rosenthal remarked, jazz had become 'a nostalgia trip, and the boundary between celebrating jazz and embalming it is not always very clear'. In London's multi-level record stores like Oxford Street's Virgin Megastore, where you could find the remastered-for-CD-fidelity Blue Note reissues imported from Japan, jazz was literally *walled off* from other parts of the store: a separate, soundproofed listening room and 'get the fuck out' glances directed at those who looked like they lacked the means or manners.[5] The Blue Note coffee table books had began to appear. Jazz was being *preserved*, entombed in the sepia of a Ken Burns documentary. 'America's classical music', that Eurocentric frame; and, at the close of the Cold War, its groove-jumping and dissonant post-war pathways smoothed into a soundtrack to America's said-to-be inevitable, post-Civil Rights triumph.

But for some, jazz would retain its edge into what became trip-hop. Charlie Dark remembered hearing Peterson and Forge DJ at Dinqwalls.

> Walking into that building and hearing jazz played at high volume on a booming crystal-clear system changed my life forever and buried somewhere in my archive is a tape I taped

on my Walkman of that very first session. A dark room, filled with dancers and Herbie Hancock and the Headhunters "Sly" on the system was the catalyst for a twenty year exploration into jazz and all of its avenues.

Dark had grown up with his mother's 'record collection to die for. Curtis Mayfield, Marvin Gaye, James Brown, Fela, King Sunny Ade', borne of her upbringing in Ghana and time in New York before settling in London.

As D'Afro, Dark formed Attica Blues with co-producer Tony Nwachukwu and singer Roba El-Essawy. They were hastily thrown together after James Lavelle – still working at Honest Jon's – asked Dark to produce a track. El-Essawy showed up at the studio at a friend's suggestion:

> Charlie came into the booth and said he and Tony were going to play a track and I should just sing something over. The words 'Contemplating Jazz'. So I did. I saw arms flinging in the air and heads nodding. When I was done my ad lib, cool as anything, we parted. Didn't hear a thing from them for ages. Then Charlie called and asked me to meet him at Oxford Circus Station, where he gave me a copy of the EP *Vibes, Scribes and Dusty 45s*.

For Attica Blues, jazz wasn't just a source of samples. Dark had 'a fascination with complex rhythms and jazz and my drum machine were a match made in heaven'. The group's name suggested their intent: *Attica Blues* (1972) was a soulful and blisteringly funky protest album by avant-garde jazz saxophonist Archie Shepp. Attica Blues' remixes – of their own work and others – were infused with jazz's complexity and restlessness.

Their debut self-titled album, from 1997, stands out from the era's textural cool with a caustic edge. Yet 'Contemplating Jazz' and second single 'Blueprint' intoxicatingly capture that early, London, Mo' Wax, phase of the music. Both tracks have the spacious mix of a giant club; and the off-kilter coalition of samples pulled from deep crates with a jazz ear. Roba El-Essawy's voice has a kind of regal gloss – all warmth and vibrato – but it's a drifting, formless vocal, jazzy as in *lounge*. Woozy, meandering, the aural equivalent of a lava lamp, 'Blueprint' has a slightly boozy sample that balloons around the mix: it's dated, it grows on you, you forget it for a few years, it grows on you, and anyway now it evokes the era perfectly. London, 1995.

Essential acid jazz crossover records

- Dream Warriors, 'My Definition of a Boombastic Jazz Style (The Next Definition Young Disciples Mix)' (1990)
- DJ Krush (remix), 'Just Wanna Touch Her (Stoned Jazz Mix)' (1991)
- Young Disciples, 'Step Right on – Dub' (1991)
- Sade, 'Feel No Pain (Nellee Hooper Remix)' (1992)
- Soul II Soul, 'Intelligence (Jazzie II Guru Mix)' (1992)
- Subterraneans, 'Taurus Woman' (1993)
- Jhelisa, 'Friendly Pressure' (1994)
- Leena Conquest and Hip Hop Finger, 'Boundaries' (1994)
- United Future Organization, 'Moondance (Moon Chant: Hip Sensibility Mutates …)' (1992)

Essential listening

- Various, *Royaltie$ Overdue* (Mo'Wax, 1994)
- Attica Blues, *Attica Blues* (Mo'Wax, 1997)
- Luke Vibert, *Big Soup* (Mo'Wax, 1997)
- Jhelisa, *Galactica Dub EP* (Dorado, 1995)
- Morcheeba, *Who Can You Trust?* (Indochina, 1996)
- Smoke City, *Flying Away* (Jive, 1997)
- Esthero, *Breath From Another* (Work, 1998)
- LAL, *Warm Belly High Power* (Public Transit, 2004)
- Funki Porcini, *Hed Phone Sex* (Ninja Tune, 1995)
- 9 Lazy 9, *Paradise Blown* (Ninja Tune, 1994)

Also recommended

- Various, *The Rebirth of Cool* vols 1–5 (4th & Broadway, 1991–1995) [UK editions]
- Cath Coffey, *Mind The Gap* (Island, 1997)
- Rickie Lee Jones, *Ghostyhead* (Reprise, 1997)
- Greentea Peng, *Rising* (Different, 2019)
- Sharada Shashidhar, *Rahu* (Leaving, 2020)
- Witch Prophet, *DNA Activation* (Heart Lake Records, 2020)
- Morcheeba, *Big Calm* (Indochina, 1999)
- Up, Bustle & Out, *The Breeze Was Mellow (As the Guns Cooled in The Cellar)* (Ninja Tune, 1994)
- London Funk Allstars, *London Funk Volume One* (Ninja Tune, 1995)
- Red Snapper, *Making Bones* (Warp, 1998)
- Wagon Christ, *Throbbing Pouch* (Rising High, 1995)
- Wagon Christ, *Musipal* (Ninja Tune, 2001)
- Mr Scruff, *Keep It Unreal* (Ninja Tune, 1999)

7   Abstract hip-hop

*Golden age hip-hop – Prince Paul – sampling – DJ Shadow –
La Funk Mob – Mo' Wax goes ham – Dan the Automator –
Bambaataa's aesthetic*

In his *Straight No Chaser* column, Mo' Wax founder James
Lavelle refuted the trip-hop label, describing artists Nightmares
on Wax, the Dust Brothers, RPM and DJ Shadow as 'abstract hip-
hop'. *Abstract* – suggesting something beyond what the lyrics
meant. And something more searching, deconstructed, *cooler*,
than sleepy repetitive beats and loops. But it would suggest,
too, what the music took from hip-hop, and what it took away.

Lavelle was 18 when, in 1993, he and Gilles Peterson started
That's How It Is on Monday nights at Bar Rumba on London's
Shaftesbury Avenue.

> It was dark, it was underground, it was smokey. Bass-heavy.
> And people were not focused on the DJ so much; they were
> really just dancing and letting go and there was this sort of
> spirit of this great eclecticism and feeling that you could
> really go on a journey and these records kind of allowed
> you to go in these new places, with new sounds. More
> soundtracky. A new way of hearing hip-hop that fitted in
> between all of the jazz and the soul and the funk and the
> eclecticism of hip-hop.

Through his record store jobs and his *Straight No Chaser*
column, Lavelle cultivated relationships with record dealers
and label contacts, including at key labels in American

hip-hop: Tommy Boy, Elektra, Wild Pitch. 'I was getting a lot of these records before anyone else', he remembered. 'Gang Starr, De La, Pete Rock, Brand Nubian, this amazing period of – Tribe Called Quest – of the golden days of hip-hop'.

He remembered playing Jeru The Damaja's 'Come Clean', produced by DJ Premier, taking its weird, spectral, watery, percussive sample from jazz percussionist Shelly Manne's 1973 *Mannekind* (the album's liner notes credit 'ray gun, whistles, siren ring, sheet of tin').

> When you got a record like this, it was just *mad* how it would go down. Place would just go nuts…. This was a total game-changer, the production on this record.

These were the records of hip-hop's 'golden age'. By the late 1980s, sampling had extended hip-hop's palette beyond its foundational funk and jazz-funk breakbeats and into all genres of American popular music. In 1984, producer Marley Marl had accidentally captured a snare sound on a E-mu Emulator, one of the first (relatively) affordable and portable samplers. The snare sounded better than the one available on the drum machines then peppering the electro records he was producing. Nate Patrin describes the implications in his book *Bring That Beat Back: How Sampling Built Hip-Hop*:

> The epiphany hit Marl that if he could isolate a beat like that, he could do that for any drum sound he wanted – a kick, a hi-hat, a snare – and from any drummer he wanted. If he wanted to rebuild an entirely new drum pattern from an old funk single, he could do so, in a far more granular and individualistic style than just looping a beat could.

Sampling like this allowed something more sophisticated than high-wire turntable virtuosity, tape pausing, drum machine programming, or spooling tape loops around a studio. Marl's beats were soon in rivalry with those from producers including Cedric 'Ced-Gee' Miller, whose virtuosity with an E-mu SP-12 involved 'chopping' a sample into components and reordering them in mesmerizing loops.

The beginning of that 'golden-age' is epitomized in the abundant sample-craft of three albums of 1988–Public Enemy's *It Takes A Nation of Millions to Hold Us Back*, produced by the Bomb Squad; the Beastie Boys' *Paul's Boutique*, produced by the Dust Brothers; and De La Soul's *3 Feet High and Rising*, produced by Prince Paul.

There's an argument to be made that Prince Paul invented trip-hop and got little of the credit – or the blame. 'Distilled bizarritude', Andy Pemberton's phrase from the article that coined the genre, might describe something of Prince Paul's sensibility, which spans goofy humour and a dark, jagged, languid melancholy. *3 Feet High and Rising* sampled classic soul, rhythm & blues, doo-wop, disco and funk, all in abundance and fluidity: everything from old-school hip-hop to Johnny Cash to *Snow White and the Seven Dwarfs*. Paul would be an influence and a mentor to many, including the Wu-Tang Clan's RZA – with whom he would be a part of early-1990s deconstructed spectral hip-hop concept group Gravediggaz. Of Paul's influence, RZA commented, 'he did show everybody that you could take anything with a sampler – cartoons, children's records, French lessons – and make it musical'.

The few short years ahead saw ever-more-innovative sample-based production which enabled ever-more-fluid and rhythmically complex rapping. In the work of producers like Pete Rock, DJ Premier, Large Professor, Q-Tip, Diamond D – and, later, Madlib and J Dilla – source records were chopped, sliced, slowed, sped, reversed, rerecorded, recontextualized and variously reenacted and reanimated. Hip-hop producers didn't need the permission of 'plunderphonics' theorists; all it took was ingenuity, punishing hours, adaptive virtuosity and amazing creativity.

A hip-hop producer with a sampler was in a relentlessly competitive and innovative craft, as had been the dub engineer at a mixing desk on a Friday night. Producers pushed deep into music history, seeking out a sample's source – some of them would remain mysterious for years – and, as Thes One recalled, 'it wasn't just what the sample was. We would find the original record and then we'd go alright, who played on it? Who produced it? What label was it on? Are there other records that sound like this?'

Copyright litigation would presently ravage sample-based production – the $1.7 million lawsuit against De La Soul; the 1991 *Grand Upright Music, Ltd. v. Warner Bros. Records Inc.* decision against Biz Markie. Albums like *3 Feet High and Rising* or *Paul's Boutique*, which were made of *hundreds* of samples, became prohibitively complex and expensive to make. Pete Rock, who in the early 1990s developed a production style rich in jazz inflections – horns like passing clouds, moody low-pass filtered basslines, vibraphones and electric pianos in suffusing warmth – recalled:

> There are a lot of things I passed up that I wanted to just loop, but I knew they would come after me for it. And they always get what they want. Certain artists like James Brown now get, like, fifty, sixty percent of a song – of your song.

But this pushed producers to further ingenuity. Some had segments re-recorded and credited to live performers. Pete Rock said, 'I find a lot of obscure music where the group ain't around no more, or cats don't know the music when they hear it. But I don't sample it to where they can notice it. I chop it up and do certain things to it so it doesn't sound the same'.

Among the records that Lavelle wrote about for *Straight No Chaser* was 'Doin' Damage In My Native Language (Shadow's Legitimate Mix)'. The song was a remix of African hip-hop group Zimbabwe Legit, on Hollywood BASIC, Disney's short-lived hip-hop label. The remix – by 'Shadow' – bore little resemblance to the original. It was built around a sample of jazz drummer Idris Mohammed, and it sampled hip-hop, funk (The Fatback Band), jazz, Canadian gospel rock band Ocean, Steely Dan, Gil Scott-Heron, Muhammad Ali, Richard Pryor … and more. It seemed to Lavelle a clear break from the 'cut & paste' style of hip-hop instrumentals of the time. 'Hearing this record, it just blew my mind. … I heard this and it was sort of the same feeling that I got when I first heard Massive Attack. It just had this very unique thing about it'.

DJ Shadow was Josh Davis. He grew up in small-town Davis, some twenty miles from California's state capital Sacramento – neither place a cultural hub for hip-hop. Davis had figured out hip-hop's DJ craft by trial and error, trying to imitate Grandmaster Flash, listening to hip-hop wherever he could on Bay Area radio stations, buying hip-hop records through special orders; gradually figuring out and picking up classic breakbeat records from used record stores in Davis. His influences included Prince Paul, Kurtis Mantronik and Double Dee & Steinski – 'guys who had a stack of records behind them and just let their imaginations take over'.

A self-taught hip-hop purist, Davis chose 'Shadow' as a moniker because 'I thought that producers should stick to being in the background'. His 'Lesson Four' collage record was released by Hollywood BASIC's A&R rep Dave 'Funken' Klein as an 800-copy promo to avoid copyright disputes.

Lavelle gave constant play to 'Doin' Damage' at his DJ nights in London. By the time he finally reached out, Funken Klein was in declining health and Shadow's demos weren't being picked up at other labels.

1993's 'In/Flux' was the first of a series of genre-defining – for better or worse – releases that Mo'Wax put out by DJ Shadow; and it was twelve minutes of loping, spacious, non-linear instrumental hip-hop collage. The following year, a double A-sided release paired DJ Krush's 'Kemuri' with Shadow's 'Lost and Found (S.F.L.)' – one of two releases that represented, for Lavelle, a turning point for the label.

The other was La Funk Mob's *Casse Les Frontières Fou Les Têtes En L'Air* EP – revealingly, *Breaking Boundaries Messing Up Heads*. La Funk Mob were French hip-hop production duo Hubert Blanc-Francard and Philippe Zdar (later to be French house duo Cassius). Zdar produced for French rapper MC Solaar. And he had produced Melaaz's unmissable 'Non Non Non': a supple, fluid version of reggae singer Dawn Penn's classic 'You Don't Love Me (No, No, No)' in which rapper/chanteuse Melaaz Bennacer's sublime vocal weaves amid the track's pendent bassline.

Casse Les Frontières Fou Les Têtes En L'Air contained stunning techno remixes of the duo's singles from Carl Craig and Richie Hawtin. Hawtin's track – 'Motor Bass Get Phunked Up (Electrofunk Remix)'– takes the coiled, threadbare drama of the original and vaults it, great piston nights, into something still stunning in its pounding, revolving bass sound and spackled, pneumatic snare.

It was the embrace of hip-hop that took Mo' Wax to the next level of ambition. With incoming art directors Will Bankhead and Ben Drury, Lavelle was inspired by the full aesthetic – music, fashion, community, lifestyle – of hip-hop labels like Def Jam and Tommy Boy. Swifty's hand-drawn acid jazz–scene 'typografix' gave way to full-bleed cover art from graffiti artists including Brighton-based Req One, 3D (Massive Attack's Robert Del Naja) and legendary New York artist Futura 2000. 3D designed the label's crushingly expensive, brilliantly expansive *Headz* collections. Mo' Wax's sleeves now featured gatefolds, coloured vinyl, even picture discs.

'James just went *ham* on the packaging and the design', says Charlie Dark, of Attica Blues: 'everything that contributed to the moment that you picked the record up in the record store had been thought about'.

Among them were the monster triple LP *Dr. Octagon*, a collaboration between San Francisco hip-hop producer Dan the Automator and former Ultramagnetic MCs member Kool Keith. For Automator, the project was an attempt to return to the eclecticism of hip-hop in the 1980s. For Keith it was 'sci-fi, science and sex. And cannibalism, mixed'.

Automator had his start with 'Lessons'-style beat collage too. Later, he and Prince Paul would hit it off with their Handsome Boy Modeling School project: a group that started as a joke and ended with sold-out tours and spin-off characters. Automator's influence is inescapable in later trip-hop stylists like Wax Tailor and The Sound Defects. (Automator's production is why some people will say the first *Gorillaz* album is trip-hop.)

Mo' Wax put out a double LP of *Instrumentalyst* (*Octagon Beats*), too – so that DJs could spin Automator's sometimes-brisk-sometimes-stoned production: the album's crisp, gritty boom-bap snares, ghostly textures, woebegone violin, and the unearthly wah-wah turntablism of virtuoso DJ Qbert.

Shadow knew he was a poor fit for the early Mo'Wax roster. His next release, the thirty-four-minute 'What Does Your Soul Look Like' was conceived in opposition to 'all this acid jazz kind of dopey sentimentality' and he lamented the exhausting, isolating Mo'Wax tours:

> I'd be trying to play hip-hop to audiences in Europe. And after two songs, they'd just start giving up on me. This was when really important hip-hop records were coming out, the New York sound. It was a real exciting time, and I identified with that stuff.

For his debut *Endtroducing.....* (1996), he was 'trying to find a sound different from everybody else's', he remembered, 'so the source material had to be different from everybody else's'. The album's innumerable samples ranged South Korean breakbeat records to Björk's 'Possibly Maybe' to Roger Waters and Ron Geesin's 'Seven Dwarves in Penis Land' to psych-soul band Rotary Connection to John Carpenter films to producer David Axelrod's jazz fusion adaptation of William Blake's eighteenth-century poetry.

Everything on the album is sampled. The album never lacks direction, funk; it is a masterpiece of sustained tension. Yet it is also ponderous, elegiac and thick with melancholy, accumulative, gorgeous and rich in texture. It *feels* smooth and accessible, yet has the bombastic sound poetry of its impeccably resonant drum samples. *Endtroducing.....* was sourced in labyrinthine record store basements and produced in Dan the Automator's tiny home studio. Yet it carries the sense of almost endless space.

For Charlie Dark, imitation of American hip-hop, in particular its narrative tropes of the early 1990s, was a dead end; and Lavelle's approach with Mo'Wax was a way forward:

> All these other people were just trying to follow what's happening in New York. And at some point we're all going to wake and realize *we are not from the Bronx.*

The instrumental hip-hop that both Mo'Wax and Ninja Tune were now putting out seemed to sidestep the long-standing suspicion that hip-hop without American-accented rappers wasn't authentic. Coldcut's Matt Black recalled, 'failing to have good vocalists from the U.K., we started jazzing it up with samples'.

Still: hip-hop *wasn't* just an aesthetic, a consumer lifestyle, the beats, the graffiti, the streetwear. It was a complete integration of four arts, including rapping; and above all hip-hop was *about* authenticity. Authenticity in relationship between storyteller and lived experience; authenticity in sampling – original source, original discovery. DJ Shadow remembered how 'you always had to throw in little indicators and signposts along the way that articulated that you knew where all this stuff came from and that you were *real*'.

To give one example: 'Hip Hop Pioneers', from DJ Cam's *Substances*, is certainly sincere in its references to Public Enemy, Eric B. & Rakim, Group Home, Gang Starr, Jeru, Tribe – sampling them before a floral Gil Evans jazz sample blooms into the song. On records like this, as on others by The Herbaliser or DJ

Vadim or DJ Krush, there were fragments of Black voices – male and female – some artifacts in the faithful splicing and looping of samples; some in sincere tribute to the music's pioneers.

But this merely exposed what was missing. For, if trip-hop was actually 'abstract hip-hop', then what it was abstracted *of* was Black voices – which is why what traces of them remained were so disorienting. On records like Cam's *Substances* or DJ Vadim's *U.S.S.R. Repertoire (The Theory Of Verticality)* – twisted, stretched, distended in their own way – are the stray, glancing, ghostly voices of young Black men, a weird spectral disembodiment oddly enacting the absence of so many amid mid-1990s' peak mass incarceration. Those voices are cloaked in clouds of static; warped through vinyl weathering; or made distant through a disturbing watery reverb.

If hip-hop's virtuosic turntablism and sampling innovations could be learned, what was harder to get to – especially if you weren't African-American – was the cultural and political context that was passing generational hands. Hear, for contrast, Digable Planets' *Blowout Comb* (1994). That album is unmistakably political and rich in reference to the Black revolutionary engagements of the 1960s onwards, the Panthers, COINTELPRO, George Jackson; to Black cultural nationalism and the Fiver Percenters; and in its celebration of Brooklyn's Fort Greene neighbourhood. Much of the album seemed allusive, dense, and opaque to white listeners; and likely remains so, even with the aid of Genius.com.

In its engagement with the jazz and funk of the 1960s and 1970s, golden age hip-hop alluded to the Civil Rights years and the Black Arts Movement. Trip-hop's use of the same rare vinyl could be texturally rich and rhythmically thrilling – but politically inert. Ideas like 'plunderphonics', beginning with a model of appropriation, *interrupted* hip-hop's promise of an intergenerational transfer of cultural wealth. And the idea of trip-hop actually insulted it. Andy Pemberton dismissed 1990s hip-hop as 'a whole culture and musical genre best left to low riding Americans obsessed with guns and girls with big bottoms. But now all that is changing' thanks to records – like Shadow's 'In/Flux' – 'designed to give your cerebellum a run for its money'.

This could only be embarrassing for the artists who were trying to engage with humility and reverence with an art form they loved. Shadow recalled Afrika Bambaataa – the pioneer of electro who brought together early hip-hop, post-disco funk, German and Japanese synthesizer pop:

> Bambaataa's aesthetic, which was basically, you should listen to the music that wasn't necessarily intended for you, is one of the single most inspirational concepts that I've ever been given. And in times of struggle or when people that I felt didn't know as much about the culture as I did were telling me that I wasn't real, I always had to try to remind myself like try to be brave and exhibit the culture with your own personality applied to it.

Hip-hop, in other words, had *always* been enough.

Essential listening

- Prince Paul, *Psychoanalysis: What Is It?* (WordSound, 1996)
- Pete Rock, *PeteStrumentals* (Barely Breaking Even, 2001)
- The RZA, *Ghost Dog: The Way of the Samurai (Music from the Motion Picture)* (Victor Japan, 1999)
- DJ Shadow, *Preemptive Strike* (Mo'Wax, 1998)

- DJ Shadow, *Endtroducing.....* (Mo'Wax, 1996)
- La Funk Mob, *Casse Les Frontières Fou Les Têtes En L'Air (Breaking Boundaries Messing Up Heads) EP* (Mo'Wax, 1994)
- La Funk Mob, *Tribulations Extra Sensorielles EP* (Mo'Wax, 1994)
- Various, *Headz (A Soundtrack of Experimental Beathead Jams)* (Mo'Wax, 1994)
- Dr Octagon, *Dr Octagon* AKA *Ecologyst* AKA *Dr Octagonecologyst* (Bulk, Mo'Wax, Dreamworks, 1996)
- Dr Octagon, *Instrumentalyst (Octagon Beats)* (Mo'Wax, 1996)
- Handsome Boy Modeling School, *So ... How's Your Girl?* (Tommy Boy, 1999)
- DJ Vadim, *U.S.S.R. Repertoire (The Theory of Verticality)* (Ninja Tune, 1996)
- Digable Planets, *Blowout Comb* (Pendulum, 1994)

Also recommended

- Gravediggaz, *6 Feet Deep* (Gee Street, 1994)
- Tricky vs the Gravediggaz, *The Hell EP* (4th & Broadway, 1995)
- B-Wiz, *New York Vibeology* (Manic, 1996)
- Nathaniel Merriweather Presents Lovage Avec Michael Patton & Jennifer Charles, *Music to Make Love to Your Old Lady By* (75 Ark, 2001)
- Deltron 3030, *The Instrumentals* (75 Ark, 2001)
- Wax Tailor, *Tales of the Forgotten Melodies* (Under Cover, 2005)
- The Sound Defects, *The Iron Horse* (Tone Def Systems, 2008)
- Brock Berrigan, *Point Pleasant* (Chillhop, 2017)
- Moderator, *Sinner's Syndrome* (Melting, 2018)

Interlude
20 great remixes

- Nusrat Fateh Ali Khan, 'Mustt Mustt (Massive Attack Remix)' (1990)
- DJ Krush, 'Just Wanna Touch Her (Stoned Jazz Mix)' (1991)
- Zimbabwe Legit, 'Doin' Damage in My Native Language (Shadow's Legitimate Mix)' (1991)
- Leena Conquest and Hip Hop Finger, 'Boundaries (Tricky Mix)' (1994)
- La Funk Mob, 'Motor Bass Get Phunked Up (Electrofunk Remix)' (1994)
- Portishead, 'A Tribute to Monk & Canatella' (1994)
- Ben Harper, 'Whipping Boy (Dust Brothers Remix)' (1994)
- Massive Attack, 'Karmacoma (Portishead Experience)' (1995)
- Earthling, 'Nothingness' (1995)
- Attica Blues, 'Blueprint (Attica Blues Remix)' (1995)
- Dr Octagon, 'Blue Flowers (Prince Paul's "So Beautiful" Instrumental)' (1996)
- Lamb, 'Cottonwool (Fila Brazillia Mix)' (1996)
- Attica Blues, 'Tender (Deflon Sallahr Remix)' (1996)
- Rockers Hi-Fi, 'Going under (Kruder & Dorfmeister Evil Love And Insanity Dub Version)' (1996)
- Andrea Parker, 'The Rocking Chair (The DR55 Mix)' (1996)
- Crustation, 'Purple (A Tribe Called Quest Mix)' (1997)
- Earthbound, 'Reggie's Escape (Attica Blues Remix)' (1998)
- Tosca, 'Honey (Markus Kienzl Dub)' (2002)
- Bonobo, 'Pick Up (Four Tet Remix)' (2003)
- Sudan Archives, 'Confessions (Velvet Negroni Remix)' (2020)

12 under-recognized albums

- Skylab, *#1* (L'Attitude, 1994)
- Earthling, *Radar* (Cooltempo, 1995)
- Baby Fox, *A Normal Family* (Malawi, 1996)
- Attica Blues, *Attica Blues* (Mo'Wax, 1997)
- Cath Coffey, *Mind the Gap* (Island, 1997)
- REQ, *One* (Skint, 1997)
- leila, *Like Weather* (Rephlex, 1998)
- Waiwan, *Distraction* (Autonomy, 1998)
- Hal Willner, *Whoops I'm an Indian* (Pussyfoot, 1998)
- Neotropic, *La Prochaine Fois* (ntone, 2001)
- Nile, *Born* (Independiente, 2002)
- LAL, *Warm Belly High Power* (Public Transit, 2004)

8 Lo-fi

Boom bap – lo fi – DJ Premier– DJ Krush – modal jazz – DJ Cam

Trip-hop might have been born in Bristol, in London, in Tokyo – but for many it was just the New York sound of boom bap.

Boom bap was 'hip-hop for nodders and smokers', wrote Simon Reynolds. 'Bap's the swing', said Ras G, heart of the L.A. beat scene, in 2014: 'break beat snares, chopping up jazz records or whatever record with really a laid-back kind of feel'. The boom bap style of hip-hop in the early 1990s was slower, a-kilter, gritty, propulsive, lurching, a percussive alternation between kick and snare: boom, bap. It was east coast music first, a New York sound: DJ Premier, Large Professor, Pete Rock and the Diggin' in the Crates collective – Lord Finesse, Showbiz, Diamond D, Buckwild.

The music had a deliberately off-kilter rhythmic outlay that 'trippy' quality. Public Enemy's Hank Shocklee said, '[W]e might push the drum sample to make it a little bit out of time, to make you feel uneasy. We're used to a perfect world, to seeing everything revolve in a circle. When that circle is off by a little bit, that's weird … It's not predictable'. With loops assembled from multiple elements, this created a sort of matrix of rhythmic complexity. Above, a rapper's percussive and polyrhythmic flow, reinvented with almost every line, further torqued the music's neck-snapping inertia.

There was a minimalism to boom bap. Sampling was shifting to something textural and sparse; and a deepening competition to 'flip' a sample in the most ingenious way. That virtuosity was borne of an immersion in technology that was, compared to the software workflows of the future, rudimentary. 'I wouldn't leave the house until I mastered the machine', remembered Pete Rock of his E-mu SP-12. As a new generation of portable samplers (Akai's S900, S1000, MPC60; E-mu's SP-1200) entered producers' bedrooms, the constraints of those machines shaped the music and created a 'lo-fi' aesthetic. With minimal internal memory, these machines could capture only a few seconds of music. So, producers sampled a record in mono; or spun it at a higher speed, slowing the music once captured. They would transform the sample's speed, pitch, or timbre; filter it at the low or high end to bring out the bass or vocals; slice off one side of the stereo mix to isolate instruments. All of these techniques might reveal unexpected qualities or leave some ghostly remnant of other parts.

Samplers like the SP-12 had low resolution, losing fidelity as the samples were captured, rendering in drums a 'crunchy' kind of distortion called bit-crushing – 'it just sounded so dirty', recalled producer Ski. 'It was a definite, definite fucking plus with the machine'. All of this became an essential part of the sound, alongside the wear of whatever record was being sampled; the sound of the turntable platter or tone arm it was being played from; the quality of the EQ filter box it was run through.

This very literal low fidelity, which was technologically unavoidable in the 1990s, is different from the 'lo-fi beats' of the 2010s and 2020s: anime-featuring YouTube videos promising 'chillhop music for studying'; the music behind zen

TikTok interior design loops. Here is the music of producers like [bsd.u], Jinsang, FloFilz, 12Vince, The Girl Next Door, eevee, hiyasu. Mujo, Seneca B, mommy, Minthaze, Styn, Tympanik. High John's 'Love Letter', helistofax's 'Crushing'.

At worst, this is a kind of inheritance of the smooth jazz of the 1980s, Kenny G et al.; tasteful earworm cocktail beats, their drifting chords sprinkled without tonal centre across watery boom-bap beats. It's nice, it's abundant. There is a crisp, melancholic tone, burbling guitars, the distilled piano loop, maybe, structured as a sort of brain teaser, clipped just sort of its resolution, loops-as-puzzles – just enough, head down over a laptop, to keep your attention spinning.

If you know your hip-hop, though, it's impossible to hear lo-fi or chillhop without sensing the influence of producers like Pete Rock. Listen to that carbonated guitar loop on 'I Get Physical', for example, from *The Main Ingredient* (1994), with C. L. Smooth; or the hazy, woozy, drifting 'Carmel City'. Or the instrumental tracks and remixes that were once promotional releases or B-sides, now available on the 'extended edition' digital retrospectives and unofficial YouTube uploads (peak nostalgia *and* micropayment optimization). Souls of Mischief's '93 'Til Infinity' or 'Never No More', or Big Shug's 'Official', produced by Bless One: a cloud of electric piano and a saxophone sample smouldering in and out of the mix. All of it mellow, thick with melancholy, a coalition of space and pressure; hip-hop's odd beauty.

When in 2005 the Adult Swim network aired *Samurai Champloo*, director Shinichirō Watanabe's hip-hop samurai anime series, it exposed North American viewers to the soundtrack collectively assembled by hip-hop producers Nujabes, Fat Jon, FORCE OF NATURE and Tsutchie. And though today's chillhop draws from many influences, in the work of these producers you can hear its delicate melodic jazz extrusions in a cloudy, elegiac melancholia.

Stretched wide and thin across lo-fi, too, is the influence of Detroit producer J Dilla. But set deeper is DJ Premier.

Premier was, with rapper Guru, half of Gang Starr, whose albums exemplify a funky, jazz-informed early-90s minimalism. Premier's work spans hundreds of hip-hop productions, including masterpieces in Jeru the Damaja's *The Sun Rises in the East* and on three cuts on Nas's *Illmatic* (both 1994); and production for artists like Group Home and Big Shug. Not to mention his production and remixes for British acts including Neneh Cherry, acid jazz singer Omar, and proto-trip-hop Bristol/Irish political rap group Marxman.

Like Pete Rock, Premier built on the 'chopping' pioneered by producers Ced Gee and Paul C. McKasty, a sample broken into small components and triggered from each of a sampler's drum pads. Instead of merely looping a sample, it could be reordered for texture, to make rhythm of melody; or new melodic fragments which arrange themselves, as the beat turns, into aural riddles. In Premier's best beats the components never seem to come to earth; to levitate, almost, above crunchy, low-resolution drums.

Ironically, boom-bap's sonic 'imperfections' are missing from today's very polished lo-fi, produced in digital workstations with all the plugins necessary to distort it at will. But the sounds and technique resonated through trip-hop. Premier's influence is audible on the drums and cross-fades laid down by Portishead producer Geoff Barrow, not least in their striking remixes. It can be heard deeply in the first albums by France's DJ Cam, and Japan's DJ Krush.

Krush had been inspired by the hip-hop film *Wild Style* to become a DJ. Things are always spinning, revolving, in his music; his mixtapes might be among his most consistent records. His early collaborations in Japan's acid jazz scene came to the attention of James Lavelle in London. *Strictly Turntablized*, his first Mo' Wax album, opens with limber double bass – an off-kilter inertia and woody, organic texture that sustain through the album. 'Kemuri' is one of the double A-sides Mo' Wax put out with DJ Shadow: its steaming, breathy momentum made it one of Lavelle's turning points for the label.

Krush has DJ Premier's restraint and ear for rhythmic dislocation, a sense of space and disassembly that is in common with dub, and an abiding love of jazz's texture. His collaboration with avant-garde and ambient jazz trumpeter Toshinori Kondo, 1996's 記憶 *Ki-Oku*, is a masterpiece. Later releases substitute a sweeping, epic and slightly clinical feel for the dusty organic warmth of his Mo' Wax releases. But they never lack a DJ's sense of drama: 'I always wanted something that can bomb hit the crowd. A simple track, but has a very complicated structure, and hits the crowd massively, even painfully'.

Trip-hop's borrowings from boom-bap – and, later, lo-fi's – also suggested the kind of jazz that would fit its melancholy, spacious feel.

DJ Krush has cited Miles Davis's soundtrack to the 1958 French crime movie *Ascenseur pour l'échafaud* (*Elevator to the Gallows*) as one of his favourite records. It was Davis's first film score; and with a trio of France's top jazz musicians and pioneering bebop drummer Kenny Clarke, Davis improvised the score while watching director Louis Malle's cut of the film.

Ascenseur pour l'échafaud marked a shift, for Davis – after cool jazz, after hard bop – towards modal jazz, which would have its most popular statement on 1959's *Kind of Blue*. The music on *Ascenseur pour l'échafaud* is sparse, searching, melancholic; and against the background fizz of Kenny Clarke's drums, like rain heard amid the tires of passing cars, it substitutes bebop's tight and multiplicitous chord changes for stasis, space, shape, texture – *mood*.

Modal jazz set its elliptical melodic designs in orbit of a single tonal centre. And because, decades later, sample-based hip-hop loops by definition mostly bypassed chord changes, so the records from this period of jazz were perfect textural foundations for hip-hop and trip-hop producers seeking something searching, spacious and contemplative.

To hear DJ Cam's first releases – *Underground Vibes* (1995), *Substances* (1996) – is to hear him working through not just a DJ Premier influence but a fascination with the spatial jazz of Herbie Hancock, Bobby Hutcherson, Lee Morgan, Wayne Shorter, Grachan Moncur III, Eric Dolphy. To be sure, both albums are self-declared 1990s boom bap. You'll hear the common trip-hop 'Pot Belly' and 'Sneakin' in the Back' breaks, and, amid fizzing lo-fi drums, the un-presenced voices of MCs like Q-Tip and Jeru. Occasionally there's a thicker and more suffusing sense of menace. *Substances'* 'Meera' and 'Lost Kingdom', both with Indian classical singer Kakoli Sengupta, are the album's masterpieces – the first its diffuse exoticism offset by the midtrack klaxon and turntable chirp breakdown.

But for Cam – Laurent Daumail – the jazz modal classics seem the preconditions and inhabitations of lament; and it can seem as though you are listening to John Coltrane Quartet's *Crescent* (1964) or Pete La Roca's *Basra* (1965) *through* Cam's listening to them. Here were austere, searching melodies drawn across spare harmonic drift; blocky, ambiguous, descending chords; McCoy Tyner's crisp, melancholic piano. These albums sit perhaps halfway between boom-bap's grace and grit and the floral lo-fi of the early 2020s.

A DJ Premier playlist (instrumentals)

- Gang Starr, 'Ex Girl to Next Girl (Remix)'
- Gang Starr, 'Take It Personal'
- Gang Starr, 'Speak Ya Clout'
- Gang Starr, 'Mass Appeal'
- Gang Starr, 'Above the Clouds'
- Gang Starr, 'Discipline'
- Mobb Deep, 'Peer Pressure'
- Marxman, 'Drifting'
- Da King & I, 'Flip Da Scrip (Remix) (Vibe Track)'
- Shyheim, 'On and on (Premier Remix)'
- Fat Joe, 'The Shit Is Real (DJ Premier Remix)'
- The Notorious B.I.G., 'Unbelievable'
- Big Shug, 'Treat U Better'
- Group Home, 'Livin' Proof'
- Show and AG, 'Next Level (Premier's Nytyme Remix)'
- Special Ed, 'Freaky Flow (DJ Premier Remix)'

Essential listening

- Jeru the Damaja, *The Sun Rises in the East* (Payday, FFRR, 1994) and instrumental versions
- DJ Krush, *Strictly Turntablized* (Mo'Wax, 1994)
- DJ Krush, *Meiso* (Mo'Wax, 1995)
- Toshinori Kondo X DJ Krush, 記憶 *Ki-Oku* (Sony, 1996)
- DJ Cam, *Underground Vibes* (Street Jazz Records, 1995)
- DJ Cam, *Substances* (Inflamable, 1996)
- Fat Jon the Ample Soul Physician, *Wave Motion* (Mush, 2002)
- Nujabes, *Modal Soul* (Libyus, 2005)

Also recommended

- DJ Krush, *Holonic: The Self Megamix* (Mo'Wax, 1997)
- DJ Krush, *Reload: The Remix Collection* (Sony, 2001)
- DJ Cam, *Abstract Manifesto* (Inflamable, 1996)
- Fat Jon the Ample Soul Physician, *Lightweight Heavy* (Exceptional, 2004)
- Nujabes Feat. Shing02, *Luv(sic) Hexalogy* (Hydeout, 2015)

9 Blunted beats

Leslie Winer – Bomb the Bass – Justin Warfield – Earthling – the Beat Generation – beats to blaze to

In the words of Jean-Paul Gaultier, Leslie Winer was 'the first androgynous supermodel'. *NME*, later, and no less boringly, called her 'the grandmother of trip-hop'. In the early 1980s she had become part of a New York art-fashion-literary scene. She befriended two writers – William S. Burroughs, the author of *Junkie* (1953) and *Naked Lunch* (1959), and poet Herbert Huncke – who were part of the Beat Generation, the non-conformist American literary movement of the 1950s.

Winer moved to London in the mid-1980s. She was listening to 'dancehall and Scientist, or singers like Vera Hall, Iris DeMent and The Carter Family, or Bakoya Pygmy music'. Her album *Witch* was finished in 1990; it wasn't released until 1993. The album suggests, certainly, dub's thick pace and bass, ambient techno, and hip-hop. But *Witch* is subversive and political where so much of trip-hop was interpersonal and introspective, most obviously on 'N1 Ear' ('I still can't get safe birth control / While some fucker's roaming the moon'). It suggests an alternative genre which was made of the same things but might have been a great deal more piercing.

Of her time with the Beats, she told Gerard Forde in 2012, 'I used to take Burroughs blueberries and sour cream. He'd read me the newspaper, we'd build model helicopters and do target practice, or I'd sit in the orgone accumulator'. (Google it.)

The target practice thing is hard to read without thinking of Joan Vollmer, Burroughs' second wife, whom he killed in Mexico City on 6 September 1951. In one of his accounts of the incident he claimed it was a drunken 'William Tell' act. There's a reference to the killing in Bomb the Bass's 'Bug Powder Dust'. Rapper Justin Warfield purposes the killing as a brag, and allies it to a *Twin Peaks* allusion: 'I always hit the apple when I'm going to shoot / So you can call me William Tell or Agent Cooper to boot'. The song is full of Beat Generation references, especially to *Naked Lunch*; and to Allen Ginsberg's 1955 poem *Howl*.

'Bug Powder Dust' opens Bomb the Bass's *Clear* (1994), Tim Simenon's third and strongest album. If inconsistent, it may be one of trip-hop's most varied and interesting albums, balancing Simenon's tendency to restless acid-house-meets-collage-breakbeatism and Lovers Rock beat-infused torch songs. Leslie Winer is among the many guest artists, appearing on 'If You Reach the Border', the lyrics recorded over a transatlantic phone line while she listened to the backing track on her Walkman.

Justin Warfield described himself in lyrics as a 'B-boy on acid' and 'drugstore cowboy'; and the promotional copy for his single 'K Sera Sera' promised 'an R&B-guided trip through beatnik culture, coffee-house jazz and the hip-hop underground'. Of the array of influences that went into his debut, *My Field Trip to Planet 9*, Warfield remembered:

> My mom would also be giving me Beat stuff like Allen Ginsberg, and I'd read that, along with Burroughs and *A Clockwork Orange*. The album became a treasure map. It was like, 'If you wanna know what I'm into, follow these breadcrumbs'.

Earthling were producer Tim Saul and vocalist Mau. Saul came from the Bristol scene; Mau was a Black Londoner who was, remembered Saul, 'as much into Bukowski and William Burroughs as he was into Kool Keith'.

Their debut LP, *Radar*, is a lost classic, rife from its opening track with cold war counterculture references. 'I'm double demented like William Burroughs', raps Mau in the thicket of references on '1st Transmission': Burroughs, Luke Rhinehart's predatory *The Dice Man* novels, half-forgotten cult movies like 1939's *The Man They Could Not Hang*, Iceberg Slim's 1967 memoir *Pimp,* Franz Fanon.

Trip-hop was thick with references to the Beat Generation. Mo' Wax label founder James Lavelle's early DJ nickname – Holygoof – was that of Neal Cassady, the basis for a major character in Jack Kerouac's 1957 novel *On the Road*. Japanese acid jazz outfit United Future Organization set Jack Kerouac's 'San Francisco Scene' to music.

Paul D. Miller, part of New York's so-called 'illbient' scene, went by DJ Spooky That Subliminal Kid after a character in Burroughs's 1964 *Nova Express* who reorders reality by means of tape recorders.

Indeed, Burroughs himself had a trip-hop album of sorts, *Spare Ass Annie and Other Tales* (1993), with music by underground hip-hop group Disposable Heroes of Hiphoprisy and late Saturday Night Live music producer Hal Willner.[1]

Why all these references to a literary movement three decades past? Some of this was a question of technique, an easy analogy to hip-hop's sampling of pre-existing materials. As Major Force's Toshio Nakanishi put it:

> I was heavily influenced by the Beats, like the cut-ups of William S. Burroughs or Brion Gysin ... I saw hip-hop as a form

> of collage and cut-ups.... In collage, something happens
> where you never expected it to. I felt a much stronger, darker
> possibility in Burroughs' cut-ups.

Burroughs' 'cut-up' method described the interpolations of other works and the introduction of chance; and perhaps it was that the analogy to a (mostly white) literary movement, with its revered figures now into their sixties and seventies, lent a veneer of respectability to the copyright entanglements of hip-hop's production. Perhaps some of trip-hop's artists could more easily see themselves in the examples of Kerouac and Burroughs (for all their murdery pasts) than in KRS-One or Kool Keith.[2]

And, the Beats seemed political – enduringly so. Allen Ginsberg's 1955 incendiary long poem *Howl* was famously the subject of an obscenity trial. Poet/actor Saul Williams – who opened for Ginsberg just a few weeks before the elder poet died – has spoken about the half-Black half-Jewish poet Bob Kaufman:

> Supposedly he would stand on top of police cars and recite
> his poetry and get beat up. And they'd be like, look at how
> they're beating that n*** down. And supposedly the term
> beatnik came from that.... I'm obviously very inspired by
> some of those dudes.

But the Beats' political stance, where they had one, most often involved lifestyle – rather, *living* – as performance; and it made them constitutionally less able to sell out in the way that much 1960s counterculture was being paved over, a couple decades later, by retrospectives, MBEs, and CD remasters. So, when London startup record label Barely Breaking Even was launching a series of DJ/artist albums in 1996, co-founder Peter Adarkwah recalled

I then thought about the whole Beat Generation of the poets who were sort of free-thinking, sort of jazz loving, radicals doing something different and alternative to what was going on in the art scene in San Francisco ... So I borrowed the name from their movement, The Beat Generation, and ran with the series.

'The Beats Are Back', proclaimed a *New York* magazine cover story. In the huge Books Etc. store on London's Charing Cross Road, you could find the distinctive black, white, and gold covers of republished counterculture classics from Scottish socialist/activist Kevin Williamson's *Rebel Inc.* imprint ('Fuck the Mainstream'): Charles Bukowski, Nelson Algren, Knut Hamsun, Richard Brautigan, John Fante, Alexander Trocchi, Sadegh Hedayat, Robert Sabbag.

The Beats had appeared at a time when American consumer capitalism was ascendent, and it's probably no coincidence that they appealed in the 1990s when, post-Berlin Wall, its ideological position was unchallenged. Yet on 'Bug Powder Dust' it sounds like posture: mere name-checking. The Beats offered models vaguely associated with dangerous, *outside of society* behaviour – but still, you know, *books* – in a way that coded particularly male. And it's no coincidence that those many writers and filmmakers influenced by the Beats in the 1980s and 1990s – among them William Gibson, David Cronenberg, Jim Jarmusch – all inspired to 'think about what's supposedly permissible in art' – were all men, as were those producers and rappers similarly seeking cultural references in the intellectual world available to them. (In Warfield's case, from his mom's bookcase.)

But the Beats were also being rendered respectable, commercially memorialized. Ann Charters' *The Portable Beat Reader* came out in 1992; Viking published Keroauc's letters;

Burroughs' books were in splashy neon paperbacks by Grove Press; there was a retrospective exhibition at the Whitney. 'On the Road' was quoted in a Volvo ad.

Trip-hop's invocation of the Beats functioned as part of the same institutional absorption. In a recycled counterculture, we masked the absence of a direct challenge to the conditions of the 1990s, just like the use of hip-hop's textures and lifestyle allowed an indifference to its Black, American conditions.

This was nostalgia, not subversion; and we got the books – and the music – that we deserved: a casual, commercial, lifestyle, backpacker counterculture, in, for example, Alex Garland's *The Beach* (1996) or Gregory David Roberts' *Shantaram* (2003). And, arguably, the progression of hip-hop culture through trip-hop and today's chillhop lo-fi beats.

And just to mention the drugs. If all of this resolved a politics of living into a lifestyle, so too did the shift from consciousness-altering experimentation to lethargy and isolation. Drug use and music have both a generative and a totemic relationship: how the music is made and heard; and how the music is perceived and represented. But few musicians in trip-hop had particularly strong feelings about – in the words of the *Naked Lunch* sample that opens 'Bug Powder Dust', 'your philosophy of drug use as it relates to artistic endeavour'. The Herbaliser averred that they were named after their producer's mispronunciation of jazz musician Peter Herbolzheimer. 'I don't take acid', said DJ Shadow. 'When I was working on "In Flux" people told me the music took you somewhere that may be similar.'

The drug of rave – of acid house – was ecstasy, a collective, euphoric softening of self (for all the tabloid accounts of death, disability, and ostracism). Trip-hop – its use of zany, psychedelic samples – implied LSD, which certainly would have been in keeping with the Beats and their adventures in yage and peyote. But 'psychedelia' records were sampled because they were obscure and cheaper to clear, not because of a lasting devotion to the politics of consciousness-altering.

But then, of course, it became its own thing – the music became, in the words of DJ Frane, 'beats to blaze to'. Here, perhaps, was a resonance to the tendency to 'disaffiliation, as opposed to direct confrontation with the status quo' that writers like Frank Kofsky had critiqued in the Beats.

As Ninja Tune's Strictly Kev put it,

> The tag 'Trip Hop' held so much promise but along the way the drugs got switched, weed replaced LSD and the destination of the trip changed course. Rather than enhancing the senses and tempo it dulled and slowed them.

Essential listening

- © (Leslie Winer), *Witch* (1993); various tracks collected on Leslie Winer, *When I Hit You – You'll Feel It* (Light In The Attic, 2021)
- William S. Burroughs, *Spare Ass Annie and Other Tales* (Island Red Label, 1993)
- Material with William S. Burroughs, *The Road to the Western Lands* (Triloka Records, 1998)
- Justin Warfield, *My Field Trip to Planet 9* (Qwest, 1993)
- Bomb the Bass, *Clear* (4th & Broadway, 1994)
- Earthling, *Radar* (Cooltempo, 1995)

Also recommended

- Bomb the Bass, *Unknown Territory* (Rhythm King, 1991)
- Bomb the Bass & Lali Puna, *Clearcut EP* (Morr, 2001)
- New Kingdom, *Heavy Load* (Gee Street, 1993)
- Hal Willner, *Whoops I'm an Indian* (Pussyfoot, 1998)
- DJ Frane, *Electric Garden of Delights: Beats to Blaze to Volume 2* (Tuff City Massive, 2003)
- Earthling, *Humandust* (Discograph, 2004)
- Earthling, *Insomniacs' Ball* (self-released, 2011)

10 Subterranean abstract blues

The Blue Note Club – Illbient – urban decay – Dark Days –
Deltron 3030 – Waiwan – grit – REQ

The cover of one of 4th & Broadway's *The Rebirth of Cool* compilations (volume 'phive', 1995) shows a young blonde woman with tomboy haircut lowering herself into a maintenance hole cover in a well-staged industrial-basement-slash-alleyway. A torn but carefully draped poster for *Reservoir Dogs* is on the ground behind her. Her torn-edged white T-shirt is impeccably clean. A Blue Note–style balloon at the cover's top promises 'subterranean abstract blues', a faint countercultural nod to Bob Dylan. Here was a clandestine urban underground as a lifestyle: music that promised, briefly, boundlessness and adventure. Yet it offered little for the people who actually *lived* in Shoreditch, in London; in Manchester's Ancoats; Brooklyn's waterfront, or the Lower East Side of New York. Trip-hop didn't cause the gentrification that was to overcome these neighbourhoods, but it helped enable it. Like music of many types, its club nights marked the literal frontier of urban redevelopment. And its imagery and texture reflected the urban tropes of the 1990s.

The Bass Clef in London's Hoxton Square offered for DJs like Norman Jay a venue for 'only those who were brave enough to go where angels feared to tread or those blissfully ignorant of the inherent dangers of clubbing in this part of the capital'. When jazz bassist Peter Ind opened the club in 1984, the area 'was very rough – someone was murdered around the corner, cars were regularly burgled'. Writer Michaël Smith remembered 'dilapidated old factories, many still blitzed out and roofless'.

But the area had slowly become home to a creative community, starting with artists like Gary Hume and Sarah Lucas, squatting in unoccupied buildings; later 'BritArt' figures Damien Hirst and Tracey Emin, and fashion designer Alexander McQueen. By the early 1990s, the area included photographers, producer Howie B's studio, composer/producer Rob Dougan (whose 'Clubbed to Death' would be a big track for Mo'Wax and eventually appear on *The Matrix* soundtrack). The jazz scene magazine *Straight No Chaser*, where James Lavelle pitched his Mo' Wax column, had an office there; so did Black publishers The X Press.

When Eddie Piller – who had started the Acid Jazz label with Gilles Peterson – took over The Bass Clef in 1993 and renamed it The Blue Note, 'nobody could have predicted the impact' said *Straight No Chaser*'s Paul Bradshaw.

'It was fucking desolate there', remembered drum & bass legend Goldie. 'It was a club in the middle of fucking nowhere. But there was just something about it.' 'It leaked, it had cracks in the wall', said DJ and producer Fabio. 'You felt like you were in a cave … It was grimy, underground. The lighting was gloomy, oppressive'. Drum & bass artist Storm said, 'It had this very low ceiling, so the bass travelled really well and didn't escape very far, so you were completely hit by it.'

From March 1995, Mo' Wax hosted the Dusted club night ('some scientific old skool sound system type shit'). There was Goldie's Metalheadz drum & bass night; Aba Shanti's dub night; Talvin Singh's Anokha; Gilles Peterson's Far East. And Ninja Tune hosted Stealth, from December 1995, with different vibes on each of the club's three floors, as manager Suzi Green remembered:

> We'd have the Light Surgeons or Matt running visuals upstairs for the 'Chill-Out' room … The middle floor had DJs, and the basement was a sweaty room with a stage that could just about hold five musicians, or four turntables for Ninja's trademark mix sessions. You'd struggle to get a drink, because people were dancing right up to the bar, to this mad mixture of music. One night a guy in the crowd just jumped onstage and played theremin along to the DJ!

What documents remain of those nights obviously cannot convey the energy of those nights. Nor can even the best DJ mixes, like the entry in Ninja's *Solid Steel* series by Bonobo (Simon Green). He remembered hearing a DJ Krush/DJ Food session at Stealth:

> I'd never heard slow, heavy music like that in a club before, with the whole room going nuts to it … It was heavy and deep, rather than fast and loud, and that really made an impact. It was the most musically forward-thinking night out I'd ever had.

Eddie Piller remembered, 'It took a few months for people to get their heads around going to that part of London – Shoreditch, as it's now called – and staying out until 5am, but eventually it was full seven nights a week.'

'Inevitably, the money began to creep in', said Paul Bradshaw, recalling public/private revitalization projects; the Lux cinema and art space. And a familiar cycle of gentrification: 'coach loads of punters from Essex to savour the Saturday night Shoreditch clubbing experience'. Then the restaurants and bars; the new residents; the rent increases. High end members clubs, tech offices. The White Cube gallery and art space in 2000.

The Blue Note closed when, as Piller 'the newcomers didn't want 200 people queuing outside the Blue Note seven nights a week. They changed a bylaw so that my half of the square became a residential area, and I had to close the club at 11pm'.

In the early 1990s, Paul D. Miller (DJ Spooky That Subliminal Kid) lived in the Gas Station, a warehouse and artists' collective in New York's Lower East Side – 'bombed out: empty buildings, mad junkies, the heroin epidemic'. Rich Panciera described the building with 'a net of metal welded over it outside, like a Terrordome type thing. All car parts and every bullshit piece of metal you could find. We would lift our gear up into that dome and play looking down on everyone for the whole night'.

Over the East River, Brooklyn's Williamsburg neighbourhood was home to Immersionism: a constellation of underground artists and musicians taking advantage of its vacant warehouses. 'The entire waterfront was abandoned' remembered Panciera:

> you could go throw a party at any time you wanted to. Just jack the power off the lights. The neighborhood was so dead that the cops would just park outside these parties and they weren't protecting them or busting them. They were just there … They weren't a secret.

Important to the music that emerged in this loose scene was bassist and producer Bill Laswell – including his studio in Greenpoint, Brooklyn; and the $1,000 he loaned writer and producer Skiz Fernando Jr. to start the WordSound label. Laswell was deeply engaged with dub's experimentalism and had an international perspective on music. Among his many production credits, from mainstream to avant-garde, he had worked with ambient pioneer Brian Eno.

As Lloop, Panciera put out a mixtape called *Bulbbs* on a label started with DJ Olive, named Illbient Recordings. Olive (Gregor Asch) told writer Laurent Fintoni that the term 'illbient' started as 'a joke to a reporter to take the piss out of him'. For Akin Adams it was 'the beats from hip hop, the bass from dub and the space from ambient'.[1]

But illbient was hardly the UK's blissful ambient house. For Asphodel Records co-founder Naut Humon, the illbient sound had 'a sort of New York grime ... A sort of corroded form'. For Lloop, 'New York chill out rooms were different, they were way more embracing of free improvisational jazz, more about texture and noise'. DJ Olive 'wanted to do something more rugged and ill' – ambient's 'muzak tip' seemed obscene in the context of the first Iraq War.

> It's like you're making elevator music to pacify people? Fuck that, we want to rip people a new asshole with something unprecedented.

Beth Coleman – DJ M. Singe – was back from Berlin in 1995. For her the music was a response to Rudy Giuliani's 1993 mayoralty: 'He was shutting down clubs and started to make it illegal to dance in bars. ... Giuliani taking fun out of the city was an amazing incentive to say, "What can we do?"' With Howard Goldkrand she founded SoundLab, 'a laboratory space where people are invited to work at their limits':

One night we did an installation where we got fifty goldfish and strung them in bags of water and then had illumination on them, and we tried to figure out whether they liked the bass vibrations.

Olive had founded a collective in 1991 named Lalalandia Entertainment Research Corporation. For the *New York Times*, Neil Strauss described –

Walking into a Lalandia party, one was sometimes confronted by a scuba diver waving from inside a giant tank of water; on another floor, large flanks of meat hung from hooks on the ceiling as a group of people sat around a giant table barbecuing steak. Large mazes of plastic and scrap metal turned other empty rooms into dense jungles.

DJ Spooky's *Songs of A Dead Dreamer* is the standout record: a vast coagulation of dub, funk, hip-hop breakbeats dragged across reggae skank, Erik Satie, fairground sounds, science fiction, of loops collapsing and (barely) reassembling themselves. It is unquestionably music designed to test spaces. There were terrific illbient records, most on either the WordSound label or Asphodel. But the deliberately experimental nature of the music meant that it did not – could not, by design – cohere into any collective sound in the manner of trip-hop.

And it only lasted a few years. By the end of the 1990s things were changing. 'Brooklyn became hugely popular and expensive', remembered DJ Olive, 'the cops became much more into your shit and it was harder to throw parties and harder to throw them on the roof'.

It was, as Laurent Fintoni has written, 'the arrival of the dot com generation and the gentrification of Brooklyn and Disney-ification of Manhattan'. Rents were going up; club owners refused installations or adjustments to their spaces for the sake of one gig.

'I think in NYC that idea of the chill out rooms started dying about '97', said DJ Olive. Promoters and labels tried to book big acts – Chemical Brothers, Moby – instead of running multiple rooms. Akin Adams: 'for a genre that wasn't quite a genre couldn't guarantee you'd have a 1,000 people coming in to the bridge or tunnel to see events'.

Urban decay had been part of the aesthetic of trip-hop as early as Baillie Walsh's music video for Massive Attack's 'Safe From Harm' (1991), filmed in an abandoned East London tower block, serving as a metaphor for domestic abuse. The decay of Brutalist architecture was a constant presence in the post-war British urban landscape: vast and grey housing estates, car parks, bus stations, civic centres. Well into the late 1990s, Ninja Tune's spectacular tour show featured 'huge video projections of power stations and desolate apartment blocks'.

Contagion, decay, dirt – *grit* – these were metaphors obsessively revisited during the 1980s, 1990s. The public service announcements of the AIDS crisis, for example: terrifying, dark subsurface images – icebergs and quarries – which followed sequestration and aversion of gay people, as if homosexuality itself was contagious. 'Ethnic cleansing' made its way into English, a Fascist association of ethnicity and contamination. And urban *blight*, a metaphor of plant disease, continued to suggest that decline and decay were the inevitable, organic result of contamination. This implicitly blamed the urban poor, including immigrant and racialized communities, for the conditions of North American and European cities a generation into, variously, post-war disrepair, deindustrialization, and white flight.

DJ Shadow scored Mark Singer's 2000 documentary *Dark Days*. The film follows a community of unhoused people living beneath Manhattan's Riverside Park in the 'Freedom Tunnel', informally named for graffiti writer Chris 'Freedom' Pape whose art was ghostly illuminated under the surface grates. The film's haunting, lo-fi, black & white palette suggests a community out of time, left behind. Its very premise invites gawkerism and aversion – yet it melts into a rich, intimate humanism; and it reveals, in DJ Shadow's music, qualities both cavernously grand and crowdedly intimate. *Dark Days* was filmed in the mid-1990s, before Amtrak evicted the community and demolished the shanty dwellings. Earlier in the decade, Jennifer Toth's bestselling book *The Mole People: Life in the Tunnels beneath New York City* (1993) depicted the lives of some of the thousands of people living in the 'bowels' of New York City.

These projects illustrated from the bottom up the modernist logic wherein, as Ralph Willett has outlined, 'marginalized groups (criminals, beggars, prostitutes) were stigmatized by images of disease' and were to be separated from 'the wholesome and productive sectors of society. Thus the catacombs and sewers of the city become in nineteenth-century French fiction the world of the savage, the sub-human and the excremental.'

Such thinking was foundational to modern and Progressivist grand urban planning. At the 1939 New York World's Fair, a diorama depicted a 2039 utopian society divided into districts of class, status, and social function. It was housed in the Perisphere, a 180-foot modernist sphere, a photograph of which appears on the cover of *Deltron 3030*, a concept album from Bay Area rapper Del Tha Funkee Homosapien, producer

Dan the Automator, and Canadian turntablist Kid Koala, told from a future of corporate rule and environmental ruin.

Deltron 3030's cover photograph is rendered with a ghostly, melancholic quality – spectral – of the kind to which critics such as Mark Fisher, Simon Reynolds, Joseph Stannard have applied Jacques Derrida's concept of *hauntology*. Reynolds describes a genre 'of eerie electronics fixated on ideas of decaying memory and lost futures'; for Fisher, the concept underlines the strange melancholic tone behind the 'culture of retrospection and pastiche' that emerged in the 1990s and 2000s, an era of extinguishing political possibilities and chilling austerity: the 'slow cancellation of the future'.

What future? One where cities were a mechanism of social regulation: broad avenues, enormous public parks, and elevated elite residential districts (the better to surveil us from) – yet the lower orders removed from view. Everyone in their ordered place; everything clean.

Grit and decay were a part of the sound of trip-hop. The sound of dirty, eroded vinyl was unmissable on albums like Portishead's *Dummy*, which came out in 1994. The band were named for the small town near Bristol where producer Geoff Barrow had grown up. He met engineer Dave McDonald and guitarist Adrian Utley in Bristol studios where he worked as a tape engineer, including for Massive Attack's *Blue Lines*. Searching for a soul singer, he later met Beth Gibbons at a government-run Enterprise Allowance job creation scheme.

Pop and crackle are evident from *Dummy*'s opening seconds. 'People were taking it back to Woolworths because it was crackly', Barrow recounted. 'Taking back CDs because it's got record crackle.' *Dummy*'s warmth owes much to *physical* media – with some tracks bounced to tape to introduce a thick, warpy sound. The result was a record that *already* sounded old, worn, decayed.

On Barrow's remix of The Baby Namboos' title track from *Ancoats 2 Zambia* (1999), grit and crackle coat its invocation of the pre-gentrification disrepair of Manchester's Ancoats area – 'the poor play in parks filled with broken glass'.

Not far away, producer Wai Wan was working on his thickly moody album *Distraction*. The city had acid house and techno from 808 State; drum & bass from Marcus Intalex & ST Files; the warm and soul-infused hip-hop of Rae & Christian and Grand Central Records; the deep house labels Paper Recordings with producer Si Brad; Rainy City label with Irfan Rainy. 'You couldn't help but draw it all in', he remembered. 'It was a really exciting time'. Yet *Distraction* is unmistakably an album, blue and amber, of urban night:

> A lot of it really had to do with where I was at the time, in terms of the location. Someone described *Distraction* as, they could really hear, they could almost visualize Manchester, the urban environment. The flat that I ended up staying in … I should have researched but it was right in the middle of the red light district … It was quite a seedy sort of area. Maybe that somehow, subconsciously filtered in.

'Crackle makes us aware that we are listening to a time that is out of joint', says Mark Fisher: 'it won't allow us to fall into the illusion of presence'. Hauntological recordings (epitomized for Fisher by London post-dubstep artist Burial in the mid-2000s) 'were suffused with an overwhelming melancholy; and they were preoccupied with the way in which technology materialized memory – hence a fascination with television, vinyl records, audiotape, and with the sounds of these technologies breaking down'.

In Brighton, a town on Britain's south coast, REQ was just one of the graffiti artists who emerged in the UK in the mid-1980s and would go on to create (or illustrate) albums in the 1990s – including for Mo' Wax. These were years before street art and community-commissioned murals became sentinels of gentrification – the memorialization of neighbourhood heroes just as their communities are priced out. Graffiti was, instead, seen by municipal governments and neighbourhood associations as a marker of moral and societal decay, of youth rampant amid eroding urban order.

REQ's recordings started to come out from 1994, on the city's Skint label. Critic Peter Shapiro heard in it 'music left to rot like the inner city'.

REQ's albums *are* a weird spectral instrumental hip-hop, but are surprisingly warm despite their entropy, the snares scarcely discernible from vinyl artifacts, percussion as pulmonary artefact. 'Razzamatazz' really is one of the genre's highlights: a weird assemblage of melodic fragments, ushered through heartbeats and breakbeats, cloaked by receding banks of harmony. It sits certainly in the tradition of Rammellzee and K-Rob's 'Beat Bop'. *One* is an album of detritus and echo; grit, yes, and crackle; of an expansive longing being throttled through low bitrate machines; of aerosol in saline mist; and of breakdancing's acrobatic joy blunted in gray air.

As the 1990s wound down, there were fewer places to hear this music. In gentrifying Brooklyn and the East Village, spaces were reoriented from a collective, participatory experience towards a one where everyone was facing a stage – facing one of the superstar 'electronica' acts like Moby, Fatboy Slim, The Chemical Brothers, and The Prodigy, breakbeats bristling out from exhausting 'big beat'.

Massive Attack were in a five-year hiatus between *Mezzanine* (1998) and *100th Window* (2003); Portishead in an even longer gap between *Roseland NYC Live* (1998) and *Third* (2008). The debut album from James Lavelle's UNKLE project, *Psyence Fiction*, would come out to unparalleled hype in 1998 but, as we'll see, signalled the implosion of his relationship with DJ Shadow, whose *The Private Press* would not come out until 2002. In other words: just as the 'quality of life' gentrification, in cities like New York and London, was picking up pace, trip-hop's key generative acts were entering a period of creative retrenchment – and, into the early 2000s, not touring.

Without spaces and communities to sustain it, trip-hop could only become, if not headphone music, *background* music. Music either refutes a commercial system or ratifies it; and the public spaces in which you might hear trip-hop in this period were more likely stores, boutiques and coffeeshops. Here, no soundsystem deejays hauling a crowd into a sense of themselves; nor long dub basslines pushing through bodies to enact an embodied consciousness. The shuddering weekend envelopments of a rave are not the same as tinny accompaniments of a ceiling-mounted speaker when you try on a shirt stitched by children on the other side of the world. If you want to understand something of why musicians so loathed the term 'trip-hop' – or 'illbient' – it was that in the packaging of their music it allowed, instead of collectives, *audiences*; and then, consumers. The music became not a means of community, but an instrument of commerce.

Essential listening

- Coldcut & DJ Food vs DJ Krush, *Cold Krush Cuts* (Ninja Tune, 1997)
- Bonobo, *Solid Steel: It Came from the Sea* (Ninja Tune, 2005)
- Various, *James Lavelle Presents 'That's How It Is' Def Mix 3: Peak Time* (Worldwide FM Mixcloud mix, July 2020)
- Lloop, *Bullbs* (theAgriculture, 2001)
- DJ Spooky That Subliminal Kid, *Songs of a Dead Dreamer* (Asphodel, 1996)
- Various, *Crooklyn Dub Consortium: Certified Dope Vol. 1* (WordSound, 1995)
- We™, *As Is* (Asphodel, 1997)
- Deltron 3030, *Deltron 3030* (75 Ark, 2000) and *Deltron 3030: The Instrumentals* (75 Ark, 2001)
- Waiwan, *Distraction* (Autonomy, 1998)
- REQ, *One* (Skint, 1997)

Also recommended

- DJ Food & DK, *Solid Steel: Now, Listen!* (Ninja Tune, 2001)
- Qaballah Steppers, *Dub in Fusion* (WordSound, 1995)
- Spectre, *The Illness* (WordSound, 1995)
- Various, *Incursions in Illbient* (Asphodel, 1996)
- Sub Dub, *Dancehall Malfunction* (Asphodel, 1997)
- Scotty Hard, *The Return of Kill Dog E* (WordSound, 1999)
- Various, *Barbecue Beets: Sunrise on a Rooftop in Brooklyn* (theAgriculture, 2001)
- Once11, *Once11 versus the Pyramid* (theAgriculture, 2001)
- REQ, *Frequency Jams* (Skint, 1998)

- REQ, *Car Paint Scheme* (Skint, 1998)
- The Baby Namboos, *Ancoats 2 Zambia* (Durban Poison, 1999)
- Rae & Christian, *Northern Sulphuric Soul* (Grand Central, 1998)
- Aim, *Hinterland* (Grand Central, 2001)

11 Black-hearted soul

Female voices – Portishead – depression – Tricky, and Tricky
& Martina – Björk – Leila – Everything But the Girl

Trip-hop seemed to resonate with the experience of depression. It had dub's spacious, reverberant range; it had hip-hop's obsessive crate-digging and meticulous, solitary sampling. It presented voices warped and weathered and alienated from their origins. All of this suggested depression's epic range, its strange intimacy, and the bewildering oscillation between them.

Records like DJ Shadow's 'What Does Your Soul Look Like' ('my depression masterpiece') – long, dragging, repetitive, entrenching, intoxicating, languorous, uphill tempos that never escape their own loops – seemed to map an immense scale against which the remnant shards and shades of daily life can make depression seem a kind of category error.

Yet, for its inhabitation of emotional extremes, trip-hop depended – as it did for so much of its emotional affect – on female voices.

The 1990s were still thick with the mythology of the suffering artist. Depression and bipolar disorder, in particular, were portrayed as a wellspring of inspiration or source material. Artists themselves answered with scepticism. 'Do you feel that you have to have suffered to write lyrics?', asked *Dazed & Confused*; 'No, I don't think so', Martina Topley-Bird of Tricky responded. 'You don't have to have suffered to publish a magazine.'

Mental illness remained intimidatingly stigmatized and misunderstood. William Styron's brief memoir *Darkness Visible* (1990) had done something to strip depression's stigma, presenting it as an immense, almost physical, presence: an exogenous entity with its own moods and performances – not a marker of moral fracture or enfeebled character. Yet as the voice of literary authority gradually shifted from male paramountcy as the decade progressed, it was searching memoirs like Susanna Kaysen's *Girl, Interrupted* (1993) and Kay Redfield Jamison's *An Unquiet Mind* (1995) that truly helped demystify mental health experiences. Most of all, Elizabeth Wurtzel's *Prozac Nation: Young and Depressed in America* (1994) seemed to capture a new generation's coming-of-age experience with depression, as the first generation of selective serotonin reuptake inhibitor (SSRI) medications like Prozac (and their attendant side-effects) were shaping their formative years. In these books depression was emergent from the functioning of your mind, the circumstances of your life, your decisions, your subjectivity in relation to your past, from your family, from inter-generational trauma, from abuse. You had some place in it, in other words: depression wasn't only something that happened *to* you. In these books' unsparing and sometimes banal honesty there was depression's endless, impermeable negotiations with oneself, opaque and baroque to others and to you a fucking maze.

Portishead's debut album *Dummy* came out in 1994. Beth Gibbons's lyrics and vocals suggested a psychological state between ennui and despair, and certainly one of isolation. 'Nobody loves me', she sings in Portishead's debut single, 'Sour Times' – the following line, 'not like you do', falling like an afterthought. Elsewhere on the album, 'Torn inside – haunted, I tell myself, yet I still wander'.

For reviewers this was flame to moth: *Vibe* described the 'suicide voice of lead singer Beth Gibbons that haunts the listener'; *Spin* called *Dummy* 'the sound of something horrible about to happen', suggesting that its 'black-hearted soul stirs up a whole new genre: disque noir' – and later that Gibbons 'sang like she'd taken her final hit'.

Gibbons' vocals *did* have an unsparing rawness and intimacy. The band used vintage microphones to recreate the intimacy of a Billie Holiday or a Nina Simone; sometimes Gibbons' raw demo takes were used. The 1 kilohertz frequency range was boosted to mimic the sound of Tannoy public address systems – 'they almost sound like they're in your ear', recalled engineer Dave McDonald; and her voice was passed through a Roland Space Echo to give it 'that flow and the sort of juddering of tape. It just gives it an organicness'. The vocals were compressed to make the quietest moments intimately audible: the sibilance, lipsticks, breaths, plosives that you can hear at the opening of 'It's a Fire', or the end of 'It Could Be Sweet'; the sound of her swallowing near the end of 'Roads'.

Gibbons's voice may have been sculpted and processed and designed; but it's wilful to believe it was not done so, first, by her. There's an agency that runs through Gibbons' vocal performances – and her songwriting, most obviously in the demand in 'Glory Box' to 'Move over and give us some room', a clear refutation of the idea that the song ('I just wanna be a woman'; 'don't you stop being a man') advocates 'traditional' gender roles. Gibbons refused to replicate personally, in interviews, the availability and vulnerability that she performed in the songs. So bandmates were asked repeatedly about her emotional state, and her voice. 'All we do is enhance the feeling in her voice', said Geoff Barrow. 'If it's the track that really starts to stretch right out there like in "Half Day Closing", then she really wants us to really fuck around with her voice…. I think she likes the idea of her vocals sounding like an instrument, something that's right in there.'

Tricky's *Maxinquaye* (1995) is for many trip-hop's masterpiece; but *whose* masterpiece requires some qualification. Tricky was still 'the Tricky Kid', the young Adrian Thaws who had been on the periphery of the Wild Bunch and then part of Massive Attack, when he met a teenage Martina Topley-Bird 'sitting on the wall … humming to herself, as I was walking past'. His original intention was a band named Maxinquaye: 'me and Martina'.

Maxinquaye (1995) was to be the album, not the name of the band. The name of the band was Tricky – an unstable, shifting cluster of identities and voices, in which sometimes Tricky himself wasn't on stage at all. His own vocal appearances – rasping, whispering, snarling, soothing even and guttered – are often hazy, background or foreground, present or dissolving, eroding at their edges. His music has always been replete with the voices of others: Alison Goldfrapp, Alison Moyet, Neneh Cherry, Björk, Cath Coffey, Francesca Belmonte, Marta Zlakowska, Mina Rose – and, especially, Martina Topley-Bird.

Tricky's first single, 'Aftermath', furls out a distorted keyboard riff dilated out from the start of Marvin Gaye's 'That's the Way Love Is'; the bounce and thump of Marley Marl's production on LL Cool J's 'Eat Em Up L Chill'; and 'Honeycoated vocals by Martina'. On *Maxinquaye*, Topley-Bird is more present than Tricky himself; their voices intertwined, roles and identities smeared into one another throughout the album. 'I think ahead of you, I think instead of you', they sing/intone on 'Suffocated

Love'. 'Getting her to sing the real heavy shit and me being the mellow, weak one', said Tricky – 'I've always loved reversing things and using the yin and yang of it'.

The effect was unsettling, to say the least. Critic Kodwo Eshun found the music 'headless, wraithlike, *unheimlich*, at home nowhere', with Martina and Tricky 'not so much singers as fluxes, perpetually transmitting abrupt bursts, human aerials resonating with the low-frequency oscillations of the city in tremulous sympathy'.

Tricky's influences ranged reggae, dub, funk, soul and hip-hop; also the 2 Tone ska/punk of The Specials ('black and white people together in one band'); glam rock via Marc Bolan; the post-punk of friend and mentor Mark Stewart; the androgynous artifice of Gary Numan's synth-pop. And fluid code- and identity-switching that was a necessary part of his own mixed-race background and childhood in Bristol's 'white' ghetto' Knowle West.

> … you've got to play both sides of the game, to have a few personalities so you can talk and chill with anybody. Both of them are still in me: the white guy making black music and the black guy making white music – it was all integrated from way back.

Julian Palmer, A&R for Island's 4th & Broadway imprint, said of 'Aftermath':

> like everything with Tricky, it was so fucked up, distorted and recontextualised, and so menacing … That's what Tricky had to do in order to express himself. He was born out of this DIY sampling/hip-hop world, which we both thought was the new punk – kids sitting in their room, borrowing from anywhere and everywhere.

That sense of radical recontextualization and recombination also informed Tricky's approach to gender presentation. He and Martina were photographed in heavy make-up – Tricky heavily feminized – for the record covers of *The Hell* EP (a collaboration with Gravediggaz) and 'Black Steel' (a brisk rock cover of Public Enemy's 'Black Steel In The Hour of Chaos', in which Martina sings 'Here is a land that never gave a damn / About a brother like me'). On the cover image of 'Overcome', Tricky is in a wedding dress – Martina as groom – red smear of lipstick across his face, guns in both hands.

His first experiences of wearing a dress 'for a night out' – at fifteen – were inspired by hip-hop, in a way.

> It wasn't exactly that I wanted to look like a girl. I wanted to look like those girls in the video for Malcolm McLaren's 'Buffalo Gals'. ... Malcolm McLaren looked like an idiot to me, but the little kids body-popping and the little girls in the dresses with the black make-up across their eyes – to me, they were the coolest ever.

And when, discussing the gender reversals of his early image, he noted that 'What people sometimes forget is that I'm very theatrical', it revealed his instinctive awareness of the performative nature of gender construction – and his delight in highlighting the crudity (and ease of appropriation) of its technology.

For many critics, this put Tricky in the tradition of British glam rock, particularly David Bowie. But, as critic and theorist Alexander G. Weheliye observes, Tricky follows George Clinton, Cameo and Prince in 'the long history of theatricalizing traditional gender roles in black popular music'. For Weheliye, Tricky and Martina's voices presented 'a black diasporic subject whose boundaries are blurred and frayed'; and their always incomplete gender performances exposed the artificiality and shortcomings of heterosexual monogamy as a 'safe haven from the damages created by late capitalist society'.

Maxinquaye was named for Tricky's mother, who died by suicide when he was four. 'I felt that she was writing through me', he wrote later. Of 'Broken Homes', featuring PJ Harvey, on 1998's *Angels with Dirty Faces*, he recalled

> I wrote those lyrics, but it's not a bloke writing them. How did a young guy from Knowle West write those lyrics? It's not a man's way of thinking: 'Those men will break your bones, don't know how to build stable homes' – why am I writing from inside a woman's head? Eventually, when I sat down and thought about it, I realised: it's my mum writing them.

There's no mistaking the fact that Tricky's work in these years relied on female voices for its emotional affect. The most effective tracks on 1996's quickly-produced *Nearly God* project featured or were co-written by Björk, Martina and Cath Coffey. *Pre-Millennium Tension* (also 1996) – punk-taut in its arrangements and still sounding like a coil of bad intentions – is most accessible in 'Christiansands', guttural bass churning below Tricky's guttural flow. But Martina's presence lends 'Makes Me Wanna Die' its claustrophobic intimacy and its heartbreaking charm.

Maxinquaye's engineer Mark Saunders had been stunned by the spontaneity with which Topley-Bird improvised melodies and delivered a vocal in one take. 'I don't actually have any written credit for those vocal melodies', Topley-Bird told Tim Jonze in 2021, 'but that is a *longer* story'.

It did become formulaic. Within a few years of the critical and commercial success of *Dummy* and Massive Attack's *Protection* (1994), there were lots of albums with feminine vocals in front of hazy, dusty beats; orchestral string sections shimmering at the back of the mix; the occasional hip-hop breakbeat mid-track; often the measure-by-measure tensions of a distinctively British espionage movie palette of the 1960s. There was Hooverphonic's *A New Stereophonic Sound Spectacular* (1996); Mono's *Formica Blues* (1997); the Sneaker Pimps's *Becoming X* (1996) – all fine albums, with spectacular highlights. And even music as dramatic Lamb's self-titled debut, or Baby Fox's bizarre and sparse *Normal Family* – both 1996 – could seem undistinguished.

Many of these acts were duos, presented as a sullen male producer behind the decks and boards; and an expressive female vocalist out front: Mono; Lamb; Goldfrapp; even Portishead in early publicity shots. This reinforced the impression, as producer (and vocalist) Andrea Parker said, that the perceived role of women in electronic music was 'to get in to the fucking booth, sing, and get the fuck out'. The visibility and presence of women as vocalists in trip-hop did something to obscure the relative paucity of female producers like Parker (whose *Kiss My Arp* came out on Mo'Wax in 1998), Neotropic, The Angel, Leila Arab, and Nicolette. It did little to reform the exclusive and hostile experience for women in the industry as a whole.

Even so for Björk, who was a superstar by the mid-1990s. Her albums of this period – *Debut* (1993), *Post* (1995) and *Homogenic* (1997) – are more Björk albums than they are trip-hop albums, which speaks to the strength and consistency of *her* artistic vision. Yet in profiles she was as likely to be cast as an emotional virtuoso – a sort of empath-ingénue – than an accomplished producer and songwriter. (*Dazed & Confused* co-founder Jefferson Hack asked her whether she had been to see a psychiatrist and when was the last time she had cried.) *Post* had co-production credits from Nellee Hooper, Howie B, Tricky, and long-time collaborator Graham Massey. Yet even though Björk recounted writing 'I Miss You' with Howie B 'in an hour', *Dazed & Confused* said 'the songs reflect the personalities of Bjork's male counterparts. These are her collaborators in the sexually charged, creative act of making beautiful music.' This lack of credit for her own work has lasted well into her career. She told Jessica Hopper in 2015 that 'I've sometimes thought about releasing a map of all my albums and just making it clear who did what'.

Björk's performances in these songs exhibit a virtuosity in musicality, code-switching, genre-crossing, breath control – there's a feeling of excess in songs like 'Hyperballad' or 'Possibly Maybe' from *Post*, as if there is an infinite pool of melody available to her; of range; elocution, even; timing, for sometimes it sounds as if she is in a different meter from even the most highly architected songs. And above all, dramatic storytelling.

Björk's theatricality made trip-hop a foundation for, much later, the subversive and shimmering blowouts of FKA twigs. Or the slyly hypnotic hyper-texturalized interrogations of gender in the music and videos of Iranian-Dutch singer-songwriter/ producer Sevdaliza: overelaborated body dimensions, mythological hybrids, cyborg appendages, blowup dolls. 'There's a woman, she's every fantasy', Sevdaliza sings on 'Amandine Insensible' – 'And no reality in one'.

And though Lana Del Rey is more self-consciously in the tradition of 1960s' lounge-cabaret singers, Nancy Sinatra, the trip-hop inheritances of *Born To Die* (2012) owe something, too, to Björk's vampy theatricality.

There were male voices in trip-hop, of course – male singing voices – and even they could be supple and ambiguous at their edges. Jamaican roots reggae singer Horace Andy: lean and searing across Massive Attack's records, his otherworldly falsetto and thickquiver vibrato too human to be synthetic, yet somehow exposing the artifice of what we think to be organic.

London multi-instrumentalist and singer Lewis Taylor's self-titled debut, in 1996, paced out a midpoint between trip-hop and the contemporary neo-soul of D'Angelo or Maxwell; and now seems somehow in a lineage to – years later – the delicate fractures of James Blake's albums; or the agonies and rhapsodies of Frank Ocean's *Blonde* (2016). Taylor's voices – flighty falsetto to blues rasp – are as dense and manipulated as his songs; and in 'Bittersweet' or 'Whoever' the bottom falls away from the song as the lyrics perform striving, exhausting gender roles – just at the edge of irony.

But it was, again, female voices that stretched and exposed the artifice of how we associate gender to voice. The sound of a theremin was a liminal presence on *Dummy*, a callback to the 1920s' imagination of a human voice extended by technology. *Portishead*, which came out in 1997, was an austere refinement of the band's sound, and it was followed by the orchestral and pneumatic arrangements of *Roseland NYC Live* (1998). Gibbons's voice was further melded to ethereal and artificial textures: a bullet microphone, a Leslie speaker. The effect was taken yet further by Goldfrapp on 2000's *Felt Mountain* which opens with a deliberately disorienting scramble of voice, synthesizer, and then tuneful whistle amid nostalgic fog. This sat in a tradition – as Sasha Geffen has outlined in their book *Glitter Up the Dark* – that included Wendy Carlos's and Rachel Elkind's voice/vocoder collaborations of the 1960s in which 'there's no seam between the organic and the electronic, no way to tease out what's 'real' and what's not'.

Still, there were limits to how transgressive this could be. Contrast trip-hop's identifiably female voices to Carlos and Elkind's 'cyborg voice' which, Geffen reflects,

> frightened certain listeners, no doubt due to its ambiguity. ... [it] seems to embody multiple genders at the same time. It lies in the uncanny valley at the exact middle of multiple dualities: male and female, human and machine, real and unreal.

This is why, I think, leila's *Like Weather* (1998) remains so unsettling and exciting. Leila Arab had performed and recorded as a keyboardist with Björk; *Like Weather*, her debut album, suggests its childlike melodic charms from its cover photo. But the opening moments suggest the album ahead: a peal of feedback and reverberation; a swingy sample from Serge Gainsbourg; a voice which might be male crooner or down-pitched *chanteuse*. The voices on *Like Weather* are, usually, identifiably human – but they are cloaked in effects, warped, slowed, accelerated, detuned, in shards, in strange harmony with themselves and aural detritus. They are wrapped in distressed Lovers Rock harmonies on 'Misunderstood', or laced through the lurching 5/4 tempo and post-punk burr of 'Blue Grace'. Throughout, the music has an exuberant indifference to a sound's origin, human or machine, intentional or accidental; and the sense you get listening to it – only improved over the decades since its release – that somehow the cultural baggage we drag into how we hear music is, also, a set of instruments also available for the playing of.

In spite of trip-hop's various influences from jazz, those moments on *Like Weather* are among the few to bring a crooner's swing and command to the music. Portishead did it too – Johnnie Ray's 'I'll Never Fall in Love Again' warped and distorted in a slurring parody. Swedish singer-songwriter Jay-Jay Johanson took the cue – his early albums are campy and whimsical interpolations of Portishead and Chet Baker.

But there was a truer inheritance in trip-hop of Chet Baker's magnetic disaffection. Chet Baker's androgyny rested in part on his looks and in part on the curious affectless of his voice, a kind of practiced indifference to what he was supposed to sound like. On Everything But the Girl's *Walking Wounded* (1996) four decades later, flourishes of drum & bass–inflected programming illustrate a restless temper – yet Thorn's voice floats above, coy and uncommitted, the music's glistening reflective surfaces. On tracks like 'Single' and 'Walking Wounded', in drawing out the relationship between technology and affect, a kind of androgynous character emerges from the music – exposing how much we are programmed to understand affect first from the components of gender.

It's remarkable in hindsight how *unremarked* were these manipulations, these subversions – how subsumed to background music. Trip-hop lasts, of course, into the minimalist arrangements and close-mic'd vocals of Billie Eilish – who has spoken out about the invasive attention to her image and body. And perhaps this suggests how trip-hop's experimentation was disguised within the familiar intimacy of a female voice – and our cultural assumptions that it be available for inspection.

Martina Topley-Bird's voice was captured with the same unsparing intimacy as Beth Gibbons's for Portishead. Engineer Mark Saunders remembered Topley-Bird was 'one of the quietest singers I've ever recorded. I had the C3000 cranked up really loud, and this meant if she coughed it would rip your head off.'

Still, he remembered, 'Despite the cheap mic and compressor, Martina's voice sounded gorgeous – she had such warmth and character in her voice, such believable vulnerability.'

Martina recalled, 'It was totally instinctive ... There was no time to drum up an alter ego. I liked the idea that the information people needed about me was what they would hear when they put the record on. Anything else was sort of extraneous.'

Portishead's early promotional efforts included a short noir film, *To Kill a Dead Man*. In the film, Gibbons's character plans revenge upon the husband who has subjected her to post-traumatic stress, institutionalization and gaslighting. The hospital scenes suggest confinement, the medicalization of female emotions, and, as with the film's from-overhead camera angles, they remind now that this was also an era in which the accelerating deployment of CCTV cameras was to make London one of the world's most surveilled cities. In hindsight, this was merely a preview of the kind of total surveillance culture which now conducts itself by tracking of our attention – but is hardly changed in its assumptions of absolute transparency to women's bodies, voices, minds.

Essential listening

- Portishead, *Dummy* (Go! Beat, 1994)
- Portishead, *Portishead* (Go! Beat, 1997)

- Tricky, *Maxinquaye* (4th & Broadway, 1995)
- Tricky, *Pre-Millennium Tension* (4th & Broadway, 1996)
- Björk, *Post* (One Little Indian, 1995)
- Lamb, *Lamb* (Fontana, 1996)
- Hooverphonic, *A New Stereophonic Sound Spectacular* (Epic, 1996)
- Mono, *Formica Blues* (Echo, 1997)
- Sneaker Pimps, *Becoming X* (Virgin, 1996)
- Lewis Taylor, *Lewis Taylor* (Island, 1996)
- Everything but the Girl, *Walking Wounded* (Virgin, 1996)
- leila, *Like Weather* (Rephlex, 1998)
- Sevdaliza, *ISON* (Twisted Elegance, 2017)
- FKA twigs, *LP1* (Young Turks, 2014)

Also recommended

- Portishead, *Roseland NYC Live* (Go! Beat, 1998)
- Nearly God, *Nearly God* (Durban Poison, 1996)
- Björk, *Debut* (One Little Indian, 1993)
- Björk, *Homogenic* (One Little Indian, 1997)
- Andrea Parker, *Kiss My Arp* (Mo'Wax, 1998)
- Crustation (with Bronagh Slevin), *Bloom* (Jive, 1997)
- Baby Fox, *A Normal Family* (Malawi, 1996)
- Olive, *Extra Virgin* (RCA, 1996)
- Lamb, *Fear of Fours* (Fontana, 1999)
- Goldfrapp, *Felt Mountain* (Mute, 2000)
- Jay-Jay Johanson, *Whiskey* (RCA, 1996)
- Jay-Jay Johanson, *Poison* (RCA, 1996)
- Mandalay, *Empathy* (V2, 1997)
- Broadway Project, *Compassion* (Memphis Industries, 2000)

- Nile, *Born* (Independiente, 2002)
- McKay, *McKay* (Go! Beat, 2003)
- Spook, *The Dusk Sessions* (Ghost, 2005)
- Tirzah, *Devotion* (Domino, 2018)
- The Bug feat. Dis Fig, *In Blue* (Hyperdub, 2020)

12 Exotica

Nostalgia – Amon Tobin – soundtracks – Cool Britannia – downtempo – 'folktronica' – Neotropic – Four Tet – SoapKills – A/T/O/S

Trip-hop had, right from the start, incorporated sounds from far afield the homes of its artists. That was true from 'Seven Minutes of Madness', the Coldcut remix of Eric B. & Rakim's 'Paid in Full' that unloosed the voice of Israeli singer Ofra Haza in its last minutes. It was true when Tricky sampled the soundtrack for Bollywood movie *Khal Nayak* on both Massive Attack's 'Karmacoma' and his own 'Ponderosa'.

But by the end of the decade, the stray melodica samples disappeared as the influence of reggae and dub ebbed. Tracks like Thievery Corporation's 'Facing East' (2002) felt like staid invocations of the exotic. The sixties espionage soundtrack samples became more dominant. And the genre was sliding into a flat, bucolic downtempo variant. The music became formulaic, in other words – and thick with nostalgia.

But perhaps it always was nostalgic. When we think of nostalgia we think about place, *home*. But nostalgia is a system. And it was a system that the music of trip-hop illuminated. At its best, it could be unfastened, searching; at its laziest, as it receded to music of the lounge, a careless inhabitation of the music of others.

Nostos (home) + *algos* (pain), as David Berry notes in his short book *On Nostalgia*, was a condition first described in the symptoms of Swiss subjects ('chiefly mercenaries') distant from home in the seventeenth century. It became a familiar condition for those dislocated in the global trading systems, from colonial agent to the innumerable displaced of modern capitalism. Nostalgia presupposes separation; and it holds the exotic close.

This was the great dispersed province of modern music that came into being long before hip-hop and its derivative genres. As Michael Denning outlines in his book *Noise Uprising*, national popular music genres were born in the 1920s in the ports of the Atlantic and global trading networks. We think of them as authentic, as national 'roots' musics; but as Denning suggests, 'aficionados as well as scholars argued over the meanings and etymologies of these new names: tango, samba, rebetika, shi dai qu, jùjú, kroncong, marabi, rumba, calypso, jazz, ṭarab'. This was all music of displaced rural labourers, migrants and refugees; the recordings conjured and captured by modern urban places and modern recording technology, and distributed across the same global trading routes that enabled those very displacements.

Later, in some of those same cities, in Bristol, Marseilles, New York, now home to people from the reaches of former empires – here second or third generations found in hip-hop a means to meld music of the Caribbean, or of North Africa. The artists and cities that made trip-hop, made it a music of dislocation, uncertain presences, lost places and lost times. This, to me, is why 'Karmacoma' and 'Ponderosa' work; and why Massive Attack's remix of Nusrat Fateh Ali Khan's 'Mustt Mustt' (1990) works; or Grenoble-based trio MIG, with singer Djazia Satour's invocation of the Gnawa music of Morocco. This was breakbeat science in a shared sense of placelessness and loss – an outline of the dislocations of 1990s globalization, scored in breakbeats and stray vocal samples.

DJ Olive, of the New York illbient scene, told Laurent Fintoni:

> We were trying to infuse samples from odd sources rather
> than using a r'n'b vocal sample we would take a Thai pop
> singer and sample that.... We were trying to get a kind of
> global feeling in the sound, forward looking feeling. Again
> this had to do with what was happening politically at the
> time.

But this could go terribly wrong. Olive warned, 'It can
get kinda cliché really quick'. Music doesn't care whether it
is cheaply appropriative; and it doesn't need to not be to
sound great – depending on the taste of the listener. To me,
the songs on DJ Cam's *Substances* (1996) featuring Indian
singer Kakoli Sengupta are luminescent on an album thick
with the melancholy of modal jazz and the spaces between
boom bap drums. But I can imagine that they might sound
like the samples of Asha Bhosle's voice (from the soundtrack
of 1981 India cinema classic *Umrao Jaan*) in new age proto-
trip-hop Tranquility Bass 'Cantamilla' (1993): voices as *texture*:
moody, mysterious, emptily evocative except to conjure
a mysterious East, unknowable, elementally different. Yet
casually containable and commercially useful.

Maybe trip-hop was particularly prone to this: its minimal
and loose template, its genre promiscuity. Maybe the very idea
of trip-hop was a trap, an invitation to take hip-hop's technique –
without its obligations to authenticity, without the Black voices
– and to create music of spacious longing from the music of
others. Something beautiful, or cool; casually evocative – with
all of the depth but none of the history, the pain.

Amon Tobin was fascinated by 'the way people from different cultures take elements of other cultures and incorporate them in their own':

> Recently I've come across a whole load of Bollywood soundtracks, which have been amazing because they've got this notion of what Western music sounds like that is just as skewed as Hollywood's notion of Eastern music. I'm quite fascinated by the misunderstanding that creates something new. If you listen to Martin Denny and all that easy-listening stuff from the '50s and '60s, their idea of Hawaiian or Eastern music was so far off from reality, but by virtue of that, it created a new sound.

Albums like Les Baxter's *Ritual of the Savage (Le Sacre du Sauvage)* (1951) and Martin Denny's *Exotica* (1957) pioneered a particular variety of lounge music – one designed to lull the listener into a range of orientalist fantasies. *Afro-Desia* was the title of a 1959 album. Another promised 'the myriad tinkle of instruments foreign to our civilization'. This 'space age' subgenre was sampled out beyond irony by San Francisco experimental/noise duo Tipsy, on *Trip Tease: The Seductive Sounds of Tipsy* (1996). But it was also the legacy into which trip-hop at its most casual, its most easy listening – Thievery Corporation, Boozoo Bajou – became lounge music.

Amon Tobin's music is not lounge music. Unlike, if we're honest, much of the mid-1990s Ninja Tune roster with whom he toured. *Bricolage* (1997) and *Permutation* (1998) work within trip-hop's space, and contain a sense of the tempo, texture, and tone drawn from Latin musics like samba, bossa, son – something that reviewers made sure to reference to his Brazilian heritage. But all this was enmeshed in the freneticism of drum & bass, a music that shimmered with complexity and plunging, pounding drama. Tobin was colliding breakbeats from big band–era jazz drum solo battles. It could sound like he was stacking houses on top of one another. 'The audiences did hate me, with a passion', he recalled. 'I had several projectiles thrown at me. But I felt, very strongly, that it was irrelevant to me whether someone wanted to hear it or not. I was going to do it anyway'.

Tobin knew that too grounded an invocation of origin was somehow antithetical to the music. 'I just didn't want to become a parody of myself, just making "Brazilian drum'n'bass" as a matter of course', he told Marc Weidenbaum. 'I'm influenced by everything I hear', he said. 'In my opinion, people pay way too much attention to one's origins.'

This is what British producer Wai Wan knew, too, resisting all but the most subtle cues to his parents' Hakka heritage on his debut *Distraction* (1998). But not everyone proceeded with such sensitivity. The early 2000s saw a casually appropriative global DJ culture, perhaps exemplified by American producer Diplo (whose first album, 2004's *Florida*, was an uncharacteristic trip-hop album on Ninja Tune's Big Dada imprint). Records produced quickly and recorded hot and available for cents around the world would be irresistible to sample-hunters. A kind of digital nomad-era 'beat tourism' can be heard on records like Guadaloop's *Desired in the 3 Worlds* (2010) who, the album description boasts, 'went to the nearest record store and got all the Indian records he could find'. The album is raucous, exuberant, tightly sampled and giddily manipulated in pitch and tempo – yet so much of it simply imparted by the energy of the original recordings.

Perhaps something like this was the predictable outcome of plunderphonics' supposedly subversive potential. Through the early 2000s, everything got easier: digital audio workstations instead of low-fidelity hardware samplers; massive digital libraries available via broadband Internet instead of crate-digging through dusty collections or record stores.

We like to imagine music as a passport to other cultures, but maybe what we really mean is a *ticket*, one which you can buy by sampling music you don't know anything about. French trip-hop band Chinese Man evoke a fictional character who 'decided to send his disciples around the world to spread the Zen spirit with old music samples and supersonic bass!' Their image is as much a boisterous hotchpotch of stereotype and caricature as their music is of casually raided samples. Their North American tour in 2018 drew protests. Chinese Man are, obviously, not Chinese.

Maybe you remember that the 'The Look of Love' – the Bacharach/David song featured on the 1967 Bond movie *Casino Royale* – was covered by the Wild Bunch in 1987: among the first of those Bristol recordings to bring together dub, hip-hop, a forlorn ballad.

In the decade that followed, the Bond thing would exemplify trip-hop's engagement with the suffusing nostalgia for Britain's 'swinging sixties'. Portishead had quoted *Bond* soundtrack composer John Barry – alongside film composers like Lalo Schifrin, Bernard Herrmann and Riz Ortolani. And by 1997, John Barry themes were getting sampled (twice) by Mono in their debut *Formica Blues*; and by Bristol duo Purple Penguin; and by Grantby, whose name referenced the movie *The Ipcress File* (score by Barry). Barry's *Goldfinger* score was sampled on the Sneaker Pimps' '6 Underground', included on the 'electronica' soundtrack for the Val Kilmer–starring *The Saint* reboot, another British espionage reboot.

Just like the pastiche crime movies of Guy Ritchie; or the pastiche guitar bands of Britpop, this was part of the nostalgia swamping UK culture. There were Bond soundtrack tribute albums and Bond soundtrack parody tribute albums. Creatively, the trend reached its apotheosis in Goldfrapp's *Felt Mountain* (2000): its soundtrack harpsichord sounds, its reverb-soaked whistled melodies, and above all in Alison Goldfrapp's processed voice breathy and bombastic allusions to the style of Shirley Bassey.

This was exotica, in its own way: these evocations of the 'swinging sixties' but with all the social conditions taken out. Portishead's Beth Gibbons saw it, commenting in a rare interview that 'it's mainly the people who weren't around during the '60s that hanker after them'.

Such was the spirit of the 'Cool Britannia' moment. Music was positioned no longer at punk's vanguard of internal anarchy, but instead one of the country's key cultural exports in a post-industrial 'service economy'. And the uncomfortable fact is that trip-hop put innovations from Black music in the service of a watered-down, nationalistic crossover, one small subroutine in the firmware for Brexit.

But it wasn't the only recursive exoticism that trip-hop seemed to enable in the UK. In what was to become known as downtempo, a true lounge style of the music emerged: dub's experimentalism long gone; breakbeats flattened out into the most predictable patterns. Instead, the warmth of vintage synthesizers and soft intimations of folk instruments and rural sounds.

An idealized sense of place had been nascent in the hazy, bucolic manner of 'chill out' – the ambient-infused rave-and-club comedown of The KLF and The Orb. Now it was present in the pastoral delicacy of Lemon Jelly's *LemonJelly.ky* (2000). Jon Kennedy's *Take My Drum to England* (2003) is a much less boring album, but its referents are clear in the title's allusion to the folkloric myth that Sir Francis Drake may be summoned to save an imperiled England. On 'East Is East' (for a line by imperial poet Rudyard Kipling), a sitar floats above the middle of the album like Indian ornamentation weathering in an English country railway station. Here exotica suggests (to whoever notices) some vague global attachment, but it operates at the level of myth, not logic. The decay is the point.

One reference to demonstrate how the music had changed – from trip-hop to downtempo – is to The Peddlers' *Suite London* (1972). Tim Saul remembered Portishead listening to that album repeatedly, its combination of 'working man's club crooning' with strange, dissonant London Philharmonic arrangements. You can *sense* the influence on Portishead's cathedralic alienation and decay. But it's not like Portishead actually covered a song. Zero 7 covered a song. They covered 'I Have Seen' on 2001's chart-topping *Simple Things*; and the song was rendered – rendered like fat to tallow – into something woozily nostalgic, more vintage than the original.

It wasn't just British music: Kid Loco's *A Grand Love Story* (1997), like Air's in-every-dorm-room *Moon Safari* (1998), found a velvety recline in the 'French touch' intersection of house and hip-hop.

Downtempo produced some beautiful records, too, amid all the music that sounded like it was designed for driving past the countryside on motorways. Norwegian duo Röyksopp's *Melody A.M.* (2001) is a classic: sweetly clubby and synth-heavy.

Bonobo's *Animal Magic* (2002) is a narcotizing and lovely melange of breakbeats, soul jazz, tender melodicism, and aching, dusty nostalgia.

Still, somehow music born in underground clubs or house parties, at the edge of outdoor raves, in the evacuated spaces of East Berlin – it now seemed a soundtrack to commercial and quotidian grind: a crisp, smooth comedown from weekend club nights; a commute home, the motorway lights in sodium glow sliding above the windshield.

As David Berry notes, 'As with personal nostalgia, the political project of collective nostalgia is less about the past than about smoothing out the present by creating the impression of some coherent identity that has existed long before'. And downtempo was really fucking smooth.

There *were* musicians seeking to explore folk instrumentation not as some kind of recursive exotica but to push the boundaries of the music. Riz Maslen released three remarkable albums, as Neotropic, for Ninja Tune. Maslen grew up in rural southwestern England, and a sense of exclusion and peripatetic placelessness inform her music. *Mr Brubaker's Strawberry Alarm Clock* (1998) is experimental without being inaccessible, pushing trip-hop out past and through its contemporary genres like big beat and downtempo lounge. Even its most forceful moments aren't without play and charm. *La Prochaine Fois* (2001) diffuses menace and wonder out of a folk palette. If it is nostalgic at all, it is an austere, elegiac, acoustic, stretched-out refraction of nostalgia.

But there were traps. Four Tet – Kieran Hebden – was on *Pause* (2001) and *Rounds* (2003) working his way out of a dominant hip-hop influence. 'Imagine if you got Kraut-rock and British folk music and fused them together.' He remembered:

> It can be three harpsichords, a banjo and four drum kits, and that can make sense … I got really interested in British folk music, and started buying loads of records and hearing people like Pentangle and Fotheringay and Fairport Convention.

The result was two remarkably experimental albums that balanced contemplation and melancholy without invoking nostalgia. Yet the media called it 'folktronica'. (So too the music of Canadian producer Dan Snaith, recording first as Manitoba, then Caribou.) Hebden's comments recalled those that had been made just a few years before about trip-hop: 'scenes come from the musicians, not from the magazine'.

'Trip-hop is the new world music', roots reggae singer – and Massive Attack collaborator – Horace Andy had told the *New York Times* in 1998. 'It speaks to every culture.'

Trip-hop's spacious template made it adaptable to contexts far removed from Bristol or West London. Lebanese producer Zeid Hamdan formed SoapKills with singer Yasmine Hamdan – a Roland groovebox in place of the drummer and bassist who had left the band. He heard, in Portishead's first two albums and in Massive Attack's *Mezzanine*, a way forward from the full ornamentation of Arabic popular music:

> minimal; the vocals really in front; arrangements that are not too of fantasy; like in the Arab world there's too much fantasy

in the arrangement always ... just a bass line, a kick and a rimshot, and beautiful vocals on it. I really wanted to hear Arabic music this way.

If there is a new wave of 'trip-hop', exemplified by A/T/O/S, or Sevdaliza, or Kwesi Darko's Blue Daisy identity, it is because the music remained fresh, and does so today, when it retained an experience of dislocation, of instability, of placelessness. Perhaps it has dubstep in place of dub, and trap in the place of boom-bap, and maybe flourishes autotune in the place of the safety and lyricism of Lovers Rock. The international range of these artists represents not just the global, Internet-enabled reach of those trends, but also the relevance of its raw, minimal, fractured template for unchanged times.

Like Bristol, Antwerp is a port city; once a key part of sugar, slavery, and finance capitalism. A/T/O/S (A Taste of Struggle) are singer-songwriter/beat-maker Amos and DJ-producer Truenoys. Their lyrics – written by Belgian-Ghanaian Amos – explore the racism and depression that inform the city's lived experiences of immigration. Their songs explore individual precarity amid a world of systems: 'Liquid Gold Dreams', on 2017's *Outboxed*, is about refugees, 'immigrants being lost at sea' and the desperate fate to 'put our faith in those who destroyed our history'. Yet they invoke nostalgia, too – not least in how these albums seem to revolve around their influences: vintage MPC samplers, 'Mo' Wax kinda stuff and hip-hop', and vintage, sixteen-bit sounds.

Maybe this is a regression through lo-fi to pure texture, modern trip-hop empty of all but nostalgia for original trip-hop, itself empty of all but artifice. Or maybe it is finding in the materials of global turmoil and disarray a means to depict it.

Essential listening

- Tipsy, *Trip Tease: The Seductive Sounds of Tipsy* (Asphodel, 1996)
- Amon Tobin, *Bricolage* (Ninja Tune, 1997)
- Amon Tobin, *Permutation* (Ninja Tune, 1998)
- Diplo, *Florida* (Big Dada, 2004)
- Onra, *Chinoiseries* (Favorite, 2007)
- Air, *Moon Safari* (Source, 1998)
- Röyksopp, *Melody A.M.* (Wall of Sound, 2001)
- Bonobo, *Animal Magic* (Tru Thoughts, 2002)
- Neotropic, *Mr Brubaker's Strawberry Alarm Clock* (ntone, 1998)
- Neotropic, *La Prochaine Fois* (ntone, 2001)
- Caribou/Manitoba, *Start Breaking My Heart* (Leaf, 2001)
- Four Tet, *Pause* (Domino, 2001)
- Four Tet, *Rounds* (Domino, 2003)
- Soap Kills, *Bater* (self-released, 2001)
- A/T/O/S, *A Taste of Struggle* (DEEP MEDi, 2014)
- A/T/O/S, *Outboxed* (DEEP MEDi, 2017)

Also recommended

- MIG, *Dhikrayat* (BMG, 2004)
- Amon Tobin, *Supermodified* (Ninja Tune, 2000)
- Guadaloop, *Desired in the 3 Worlds* (Raw Tapes, 2010)
- David Holmes, *Music from the Motion Picture Ocean's Eleven* (Warner, 2001)
- Grantby, *Timebooth EP* (Cup of Tea, 1995)
- Purple Penguin, *De-Tuned* (Cup of Tea, 1996)

- Jon Kennedy, *Take My Drum to England* (Grand Central, 2003)
- Bonobo, *Dial 'M' for Monkey* (Ninja Tune, 2003)
- Kid Loco, *A Grand Love Story* (Yellow Productions, 1997)
- Air, *Original Motion Picture Score for the Virgin Suicides* (Source, 1999)
- Troublemakers, *Doubts & Convictions* (Guidance, 2001)
- Quantic, *The 5th Exotic* (Tru Thoughts, 2001)
- Télépopmusik, *Genetic World* (EMI, 2001)
- Télépopmusik, *Angel Milk* (EMI, 2005)
- Blue States, *Nothing Changes under the Sun* (Memphis Industries, 2000)
- Kinobe, *Soundphiles* (Jive, 2000)
- Kinobe, *Versebridgechorus?* (Jive, 2001)
- Neotropic, *15 Levels of Magnification* (ntone, 1995)
- Caribou/Manitoba, *Up in Flames* (Leaf, 2003)
- Soap Kills, *Cheftak* (self-released, 2002)
- Soap Kills, *Enta Fen* (self-released, 2005)
- A/T/O/S, *Waterman* (DEEP MEDi, 2020)

13 Hip-hop blues

*Lanquidity – Afrofuturism – science fiction soundtracks –
Fight Club – Skylab – Robert Johnson – Moby – Actress*

One way to think about trip-hop is as a set of waves in hip-hop's expansion outside of the United States. Not the first – those came, probably, in 1982, 1983: *Wild Style*, Malcolm McLaren's 'Buffalo Gals', the *Street Sounds Electro* compilations. And certainly not the last, nor the strongest. But a phase that would wash in amid the dub, reggae, Lovers Rock, rare groove, acid jazz, ambient house that was already popular in the UK, without overwhelming it.

For hip-hop was too fully formed an aesthetic to be taken entirely on its own terms. Time after time, the response of young white admirers to hip-hop was shock, wonder. In its fluid and robotic dance moves; the graffiti of Rammellzee's Gothic Futurism; its production in turntables and samplers from the gaps in other records; its staggering verbal virtuosities. 'It was science fiction, Rammellzee, Futura, Basquiat, Beat Bop, The Beastie Boys', recalled Mo' Wax founder, talking about the shared influences with Japan's Major Force. 'Seeing hip-hop, it was like seeing something alien.' This was why he approached graffiti artists – legendary New York writer Futura 2000, Bristol's 3D (Robert Del Naja of Massive Attack), Brighton's REQ:

> I always loved the old graffiti but didn't want that wildstyle stuff or tag-based street art.... With 3D and Futura, there was something almost science fiction about their work, and that

imagery really matched the abstract music coming out of
Mo'Wax at that time.

The 'pointmen' characters that Futura designed for UNKLE
have served – in concept art, merchandise, toy design,
animation – as one of its few constants beside Lavelle himself.
They first appeared on 1994's EP *The Time Has Come*, back
when UNKLE was Lavelle, Tim Goldsworthy (a friend since his
schooldays in Oxford, and deeply involved in the early Mo'Wax
years), and Masayuki Kudo from Major Force.

The Time Has Come is ponderous, bassy, moody, zany,
soundtracky 1990s UK instrumental hip-hop, built from the
crates of rare groove DJs. Billed as 'a tribute to Sun-Ra and all
things fucked up', the opening track 'If You Find Earth Boring' is
fourteen minutes long, and has little of the spiritual reach and
soul of Sun Ra's 1978 *Lanquidity*, which it samples.

Gilles Peterson remembered *Lanquidity* being 'almost like a
weekly play' at his That's How It Is nights with James Lavelle at
Bar Rumba, just after the rare groove and the acid jazz phase:
'we want to go a bit more abstract … more minimal and out'.

Sun Ra had died in 1993: a five-decade career with over 100
albums, poetry, film – including *Space Is the Place* (1974). That
film, and Sun Ra's cosmology at large, already had a central place
in what was to become known as Afrofuturism. That term first
appeared in 1994 in a series of interviews that critic Mark Dery
conducted with writers Samuel R. Delany, Greg Tate, Tricia Rose.
The interviews explored the means by which Black diaspora
artists – from 'a community whose past has been deliberately
rubbed out' – might 'imagine possible futures'. And, as Greg Tate

outlined, 'the way in which being black in America is a science fiction experience': abduction, 'thrusting someone into an alien culture', alienation from society, subjugation to power structures that suppress and delude of one's lived reality.

In the UK, *The Last Angel of History* came out in 1996, a remarkable documentary/poem/manifesto/genealogy from the Black Audio Film Collective that outlined a Pan-African technologism. The film's fractured and dislocated music, by Trevor Mathison, accompanies its restless provocations ('sonic warfare, sonic Africa, Afrofuturism, digitized diaspora, analog ecology'), and is somehow consolatory and optimistic in its tone.

The film traces 'a Black secret technology' out from the 1930s Delta blues musician Robert Johnson. It suggests that 'the first touch of science fiction came when Africans began playing drums to cover distance. Water carried the sound of the drums; and sound covered the distance between the old and the new world'. The film's musical genealogy includes Sun Ra, Lee 'Scratch' Perry, George Clinton; and hip-hop; and the Detroit techno of Juan Atkins and Derrick May and Carl Craig; the hip-hop/dub/ambient combinations DJ Spooky; the drum & bass of Goldie.

Theorist and critic Kodwo Eshun's book *More Brilliant than the Sun: Adventures in Sonic Fiction* followed in 1998, and included, too, Dr. Octagon, Gravediggaz, Tricky and Martina.

The Afrofuturist genealogy includes writers like Octavia Butler and Samuel R. Delany and Ishmael Reed. And Black visual artists like Basquiat and Rammellzee and Blade. Greg Tate noted Futura 2000's painting *The Good, the Bad, and the Ugly*, which 'pays homage to the hip-hop group Cypress Hill, has three ghostly figures floating on what appears to be a TV screen hovering over a dark, ominous cityscape'. (Look at those three figures and you see the ancestors of UNKLE's pointmen.)

Almost everyone involved in trip-hop was sincere in their appreciation – reverence, even – for the Black origins of their music. It was certainly among the many reasons that the trip-hop label was so forcefully rejected. But if Sun Ra's work was 'fucked up', 'psychedelic' and 'out there', it could be absconded into pure texture as if in a shrug, a sample, a casual reference. This is what categories, labels, are good at: to forestall deeper inquiry as unnecessary: to contain expression rather than allowing it to bloom into wonder.

Afrofuturism imagines multiple, Black-centred, futures from engagement with an actual disastrous past. But the familiar futures of the 1990s extrapolated a remarkably conformist dystopia from a fantastical past: one of supposed ethical and inevitable technological progress.

Trip-hop was popular music of the 1990s, and so it was inevitable it would be on the era's soundtracks. Tricky's 'Overcome' was part of the degraded urban noir of *Strange Days* (1995) with its prescient digital black markets. And the music was present – central, even – to the confirmation bias fantasies of movies like *Fight Club* and *The Matrix*. In that movie Rob Dougan's 'Clubbed to Death (Kurayamino Variation)' drops its soullessly pneumatic rhythm – a great record, but one that flattens the funk out of the great Skull Snaps break – alongside the film's mechanical revelations.

David Fincher's 1999 film adaptation of *Fight Club* featured music by the Dust Brothers, who had produced the Beastie Boys' sample-rich *Paul's Boutique* back in 1989. The film's uneasy satire of thwarted masculinity seems, now, to have been wholly claimed as a sort of bitter precursor of incel rage. Its soundtrack is, like the film, wittier than you might remember. But it now seems like another stop on trip-hop's journey from a joyous emergent collective consciousness – towards instead a headphone music for quiet and incoherent radicalization.

Collectively these futures became a kind of exoreality into which the digital innovations of the following years would be imagined – the panopticon business models of a Facebook or a Google; the second-hand experience of Instagram; YouTube's now endemic red-pillism.

And so perhaps it was no surprise, as the decades' futures were closed off, that the music could be so melancholic. For trip-hop, even in its futures, was nostalgic. If trip-hop had been in conversation with the 1950s – the Beatnik poets, Blue Note, the theremins of *The Thing from Another World* (1951) and *The Day the Earth Stood Still* (1951) – it was also in conversation with science fiction which was in conversation with the 1950s. The Saturday morning serials of *Star Wars*; the mourning for the mourning of the frontier of *2001*; the noir of *Neuromancer* and *Blade Runner* – all of which were influences, some sampled.

Skylab were one of trip-hop's attempted 'supergroup' concepts: Mat Ducasse, Howie B, and – from Major Force – Masayuki Kudo and Toshio Nakanishi. 'The skylab' was the 'ad-hoc noise and tape room' in Ducasse's North London attic. The sound of Skylab was inspired by 'the psychedelic and space age 60s', Coldcut's Solid Steel radio mixes, psychedelic drugs and the 'sudden flood of obscure and out-there vinyl into second hand shops' as the industry shifted to CDs.

The group's name evokes the NASA space station that disintegrated in 1979. *#1*, released in 1994, opens as a frayed version of the plasticine, portentous synthesizer tones of

1970s science-fiction movies like *Phase IV* (1974; score by Brian Gascoigne) and *Dark Star* (1974; John Carpenter), or – obviously – Vangelis's *Blade Runner* itself. There is space age detritus; intimations of sirens and coyote cries somehow coaxed from turntable cross-fades and Indian flute; lush Bond villain strings; washes of surfy guitar amid galactic burpy synth bass. The album is a mix of sound experimentation, ambient and crisp hip-hop breakbeats. But the overall effect is of a frayed Cold War mood collage.

Melancholy. Tricky called his first single 'Aftermath (Hip Hop Blues)'. In some of trip-hop's best music it did recall something of delta blues – like Robert Johnson's recordings, voices stretched and scattered across spare, unforgiving arrangements; the erosions of recording technology; speed distortion that casts our sense of the human back and forth across the uncanny valley; tendrils of dissembled accompaniment; a lulling inertia. I hear this in guitarist Ben Harper's 'Whipping Boy', spectral and murky in the Dust Brothers' remix; in so much of Tricky's music; in Portishead's rangey remix of Massive Attack's 'Karmacoma'.

Johnson – the 1930s blues musician with whom *The Last Angel of History* opens – was no less a figure of obsession for white British musicians and critics in the 1990s than he had been after the release of 1961's *King of the Delta Blues Singers*. So perhaps it shouldn't be surprising that Johnson beckoned somehow at the beginning and end of trip-hop. 'Johnson' is the first track on Kruder & Dorfmeister's rediscovered/ redeveloped LP *1995*, its treatment of Johnson's 'Sweet Home Chicago' released in odd ghostly nostalgia at the height of the COVID-19 pandemic in 2020.

At its bluesiest trip-hop sat close to the dub blues of Little Axe, former Sugarhill house guitarist Skip McDonald with English dub producer Adrian Sherwood. This was a formula that could be taken to extremes, obviously; and it would be, by Moby, in 1999. Trip-hop was dead, but *Play* was the album that evacuated the graveyard and erected itself as a sepulchre to commercial extremism. With all the charm of the luxury box set it seemed to have been sampled from, *Play* doused curiosity or wonder with a stolid, inert, personal nostalgia – even though its emotional affect is mostly drawn from the voices of the long-dead singers it sampled from Alan Lomax's *Sounds of the South* field recordings. Their names were Roland Hayes, Bessie Jones and Vera Hall. *Play* was ubiquitous in its gaudy, opportunistic license-everything to-everyone-all-the-time ethic. Over 100 licenses signed: every track on the album. 'It was very short-lived, but we made a lot of money', a representative of Moby's label recalled.

'The fact that I was a white kid from the 20th century sampling African-American vocals from the early 20th century had never even crossed my mind', Moby told the *New York Times*. 'In the long, nonillustrious history of white people pilfering African American culture, have I just perpetuated that? I'm motivated by a love for the music and by a love of the performances, and I really hope I haven't done anything bad.'

Perhaps something of trip-hop feels alive today in the Cuban/Yoruban/French beat-driven music of Ibeyi; or in violinist Sudan Archives's *Sink* (2018) – minimalist, bassy, influenced by African electronic music. In FKA twigs' remarkable *LP1* (2014) and *Magdalene* (2019). Or via its shared DNA with the 2010s'

Los Angeles 'beat scene' that include Ras G and Georgia Anne Muldrow and Flying Lotus. If so, this is because of the array of futures refracted out by Afrofuturism – in popular music alone, by Missy Elliott, Erykah Badu, Janelle Monáe, and many others.

Looking back to trip-hop with such a perspective suggests an alternative genealogy to further erode the genre's boundaries. On Earthling's *Radar*, lyricist Mau frames his perspective within the Atlantic world – Cuba, Haiti, the Arawak; Marcus Garvey:

> London is my city
> Jamaica's my country
> Africa's my history
> It ain't no mystery
> How I came to be.

It would include perhaps the Berlin dub techno sides released by Rhythm & Sound with roots reggae vocalist Paul St. Hilaire: 'Music A Fe Rule' or 'What a Mistry' ('Work the plantations everyday; great tribulations throughout the years').

In Attica Blues, the African rhythms to which producer Tony Nwachukwu had listened from childhood. And the ghastly abstract of Cath Coffey's cover of 'Strange Fruit', produced by Nwachukwu, on Coffey's barely-released album *Mind the Gap* (1997).

Tricky's *Pre-Millennium Tension*, obviously – superior in its sly turbulence to *Maxinquaye*.

The watery post-dubstep throb of A/T/O/S's 'Wake Up (Save Us)' on 2017's *Outboxed*.

The cosmic squall and crystalline textures of Mad Professor's remixes of Massive Attack's *Mezzanine*.

And such a sonic lineage would bring some of this music closer to the disjunctive hip-hop of Moor Mother and billy woods's *Brass* (2020). Or Shabazz Palaces' opening manifesto *Black Up* (2011).

Such a perspective exposes in trip-hop its unstable coalition of musics drawn from the dislocations of the Black Atlantic. It might include, too, the music of Darren Jordan Cunningham, recording as Actress, including 2020's gorgeous and unsettling *Karma & Desire* – the voices of Zsela and Sampha drawn across the album's fractured surfaces. Actress's music contains techno, ambient, house, electro; it is deliberately lo-fi. Present somewhere in his music, perhaps in eroded form, is Detroit duo Drexciya whose music through the 1990s assembled a mythology of the undersea descendants of the Middle Passage.

Actress is cautious to be labelled Afrofuturist. In particular he cites the philosophical breadth of Sun Ra: 'I can't help but feel that because it's given this Afrofuturist tag, that that's where it remains. But I see Sun Ra as much more potent outside of that. Both as a composer, both as a visionary. As a filmmaker, as a storyteller'.

In 2018, Actress recorded an album with the London Contemporary Orchestra. *LAGEOS* is named for the Laser Geometric Environmental Observation Survey research satellites, launched in 1976 – the same year as Skylab – and represented in eery halftone on the album's cover art.

The album is both original material and reworking of Actress's earlier work. It feels glitteringly modern and hauntingly, creakingly old. In 'Surfer's Hymn' the allusion to Drexciya is clear. The album is precise, blurry, forgetful; mournful and kinetic; delicate and wurlitzer. It resists nostalgia. There is in it bone and choral, fracture & beatbox; static, brittle funk and elegiac lullaby. It is a strange cousin to Skylab's *#1*, both albums a kind of refraction of the post-Cold War musics of the 1990s, ambient and techno; both hymnals to a space age made of brittle technology and brittle ideas.

Essential listening

- UNKLE, *The Time Has Come EP* (Mo'Wax, 1994)
- The Dust Brothers, *Fight Club (Original Motion Picture Score)* (Restless, 1999)
- Deltron 3030, *Deltron 3030* (75 Ark, 2000)
- Skylab, *#1* (L'Attitude, 1994)
- Ibeyi, *Ibeyi* (XL, 2015)
- Sudan Archives, *Sink* (Stones Throw, 2018)
- FKA twigs, *LP1* (Young Turks, 2014)
- FKA twigs, *Magdalene* (Young Turks, 2019)
- Ras G & the Afrikan Space Program, *Stargate Music* (Leaving, 2018)
- Actress x London Contemporary Orchestra, *LAGEOS* (Ninja Tune, 2018)
- Actress, *Karma & Desire* (Ninja Tune, 2020)

Also recommended

- Skylab, *#2 1999 Large as Life and Twice as Natural* (Eye Q, 1999)
- Little Axe, *The Wolf That House Built* (Wired, 1994)
- Little Axe, *Slow Fuse* (Wired, 1996)
- Moor Mother and billy woods, *Brass* (Backwoodz Studioz, 2020)
- Shabazz Palaces, *Black up* (Sub Pop, 2011)

14 Cancelled futures

UNKLE – Mo' Wax – the end of trip-hop – Brutalism – The Cinematic Orchestra – jazz never rests – Blue Daisy – Dennis Bovell & Jean Binta Breeze

James Lavelle's UNKLE band-as-career-as-art project has always had something of the space opera about it – not least in its relationship-ruining creative maximalism. *Psyence Fiction* (1998) was supposed to be trip-hop's major commercial and artistic achievement – but instead the genre seemed to coagulate back out into its components.

By then, Mo' Wax had become one of the coolest labels in the mid-1990s, creatively over-extended by Lavelle's ambitions for music, a skate art exhibition, art books, photography, fashion, brand collaborations with Nike and A Bathing Ape. But capital was short. A deal with A&M Records provided cash and distribution, but now there would be major label release schedules and major label commercial expectations.

DJ Shadow was brought into UNKLE. Demo sessions produced 'Lonely Soul' with vocalist Richard Ashcroft from The Verve. Long-time Lavelle companion Tim Goldsworthy was out ('incredibly slow and lazy', Lavelle said) and would work with David Holmes on the moody soundtrack to Steven Soderbergh's moody neo-noir adaptation *Out of Sight*. (And later still, he would co-found label DFA.)

While Shadow was 'a very focused workhorse' in the studio, Lavelle was relentlessly pursuing collaborations and the aesthetic vision around the project, admiring Francis Ford

Coppola's *Apocalypse Now*–era auterish maximalism. 'How could you make a record be like *2001: A Space Odyssey* or *Blade Runner* or *Star Wars*, both emotionally and sonically. But also, how could you make that record have the other universe around it.'

Psyence Fiction (1998) had improbable expectations. The commercial pressure; Shadow's creative reputation; the high-profile celebrity vocalists – Ashcroft, Badly Drawn Boy, Radiohead's Thom Yorke, the Beastie Boys' Mike D, The Stone Roses' Ian Brown, Kool G Rap – and the massive creative team from Futura to video director Jonathan Glazer. Pre-release coverage heralded a (purportedly) long-awaited fusion of hip-hop and electronic music and indie rock. There were around-the-block line-ups in the UK for its release.

The album did well; in the UK its presence was inescapable and it reached #4. But reviews were mixed. Trip-hop seemed tired and, now that there were emo indie vocals and brusque guitars, it didn't seem particularly groundbreaking. Lavelle and Shadow fought about song-writing credits. Shadow: 'I can account for every note on the record'. Lavelle: 'What you have to understand is, these are sample records. These are records that somebody's taken from somebody else. … They are collage records.'

Shortly after *Psyence Fiction* was completed, Mo' Wax – now as part of A&M – was absorbed into Island as part of the PolyGram-Universal mega-merger. Lavelle lost control of the label in all but name – including its back catalogue. 'Mo' Wax existed for quite a while after *Psyence Fiction*', he remembered, 'but *Psyence Fiction* was the catalyst in many ways for the end of the lunatics running the asylum, the crew, everybody being together'.

Mo' Wax was, characteristically, the most prominent flare-out of the independent labels. In Bristol, Cup of Tea didn't make it out of 1999. Howie B's Pussyfoot lasted through 2002. In Manchester Mark Rae's Grand Central made it to 2006 – by which point independent labels were being wiped out as the CD market's collapse took out their distributors. A similar thing happened to Asphodel, which had served New York's illbient scene. Skiz Fernando Jr.'s Wordsound survived Brooklyn's skyrocketing rents by relocating to Baltimore.

It would be easy to overstate the end of trip-hop in commercial and aesthetic terms: it was as hazy and indistinct as its beginning had been. In some ways it became – as perhaps it ever was – a pole in hip-hop's underground while the genre's mainstream ascendency continued. DJ Krush, The Herbaliser, DJ Vadim, Shadow, Rae & Christian: their albums soon featured MCs as prominent as Guru, C.L. Smooth, Jean Grae, Bahamadia, MF DOOM, the Jungle Brothers, Jeru. Ninja Tune launched the Big Dada imprint in 1997 with music journalist Will Ashon, who had covered the underground hip-hop scenes in New York and Los Angeles. Its first releases included the extraordinary 'Flohim (1972) (Part 2/25:03 Mix)' and 'Twice The First Time' by New York spoken-word poet Saul Williams. The label would not hold as central a role in underground hip-hop as Definitive Jux in New York and LA's Stones Throw – but its output would remain interesting, experimental, and edgy through the UK's grime period.

Meanwhile, albums of gorgeous collage-based instrumental hip-hop continued to come out from underground hip-hop producers like RJD2 and Blockhead; and 2006 saw the release of J Dilla's remarkable *Donuts*.

For DJ Shadow, it was the online discussion boards that identified sample sources ('snitch sites') that 'basically destroyed the art form', making copyright litigation much likelier.

When Attica Blues' second album, *Test. Don't Test*, appeared in 2000, samples were used sparingly. They were now subject to a major label's assiduous clearing processes. But the album also had glossier, higher production values afforded by 'a bigger budget, higher expectations and new technology'. Breaks were sourced from the better-preserved records that they could now afford: 'We'd done the dusty samples album', recalled Charlie Dark.

The technology was changing. In the 1990s a producer would gradually acquire a library of sounds, samples and breaks – every sound arduously crafted. By the early 2000s, there were software samplers and digital audio workstations. No storage or memory constraints enforced a low-fidelity aesthetic. Decay, dirt, erosion, warp and bit-crushed snares were textures to be worked *towards* from digital cleanliness, sample packs and digital effects libraries. Nowadays, says Charlie Dark, 'amazing ideas – but the *sounds* are all the same'.

But trip-hop's high points had *always* been an end: Shadow's *Endtroducing.....* was so named as a conclusion to the 'loop-reliant' style of 'In/Flux', 'Lost And Found' and 'What Does Your Soul Look Like'. When *Private Press* came out, in 2002, it still had his sense of brusque and accumulating calamity – but more than occasionally it veered into the smooth high-occupancy lane of downtempo.

Some artists were sickened by the commercial adoption – and dull imitation – of work intended to be experimental and underground. Geoff Barrow 'really fell out of love with turntablism in 1997' during the production of *Portishead*. Tricky had thought *Maxinquaye* would be immune from imitation 'because it was just sound, noises'. He was disgusted by the extent of its influence: 'I couldn't make anything like *Maxinquaye* again; I've been chased away from that.'

Shortly after the New Labour government won the UK general election in 1997, Prime Minister Tony Blair held two infamous soirees at 10 Downing Street, evaporating any cool then remaining in the 'cool Britannia' moment. No trip-hop musicians were photographed with champagne in hand. But as the decade wrapped the music seemed out of place. And as gentrification accelerated it was sometimes literally out of place. Among the 'cancelled futures' of Mark Fisher's hauntology was the technocratically optimistic civic planning represented by Brutalist architecture. Many of Britain's Brutalist towers came down through the late 1990s and 2000s, including five of the towers in Hackney's Nightingale Estate – from which pirate radio station Rush FM had once broadcast breakbeat hardcore across and beyond London.

In Gateshead, in North East England, the Trinity Square car park was an immense, experimental building famous for its part in Mike Hodges's coolly savage crime film *Get Carter* (1971). That film ascended, through the 1990s, from cult classic to popular favourite. Portishead's promotional short film noir, *To Kill a Dead Man*, premiered at a revival screening; the film's soundtrack was sampled into Mono's 'Silicone'. Trinity Square was finally demolished in 2010.

The buildings that began to overdetermine the London skyline in the New Labour years were not a return to utopian urban planning of Brutalism. Instead the glossy, glassy, structurally accomplished but inexuberant 'regeneration architecture' of 'starchitects' like Norman Foster, stood for the triumph of market consensus and fluid monotony of capital.

But: still standing were the Southbank Centre and the Barbican: Brutalist art spaces and exhibition centres now polished, retrofitted, and redecorated.

Perfectly suited to such spaces is the music of The Cinematic Orchestra. Jason Swinscoe, who started working for Ninja Tune in the mid-1990s, was 'trying to extrapolate narratives from film music and weave them into the tunes', gradually bringing together an ensemble to play over the loops he had sampled. In performance – including at the Barbican itself – there is something archival, *institutional* about the Cinematic Orchestra's music: it's sleek, deliberate, sombre, and expansive without being undecorative. It is music for exhibition, the kind of music you'd hear at a retrospective, the opening of an archive. Occasionally there is something rapturious or unsettling – where the music threatens to outsize its vessel. *Every Day* (2002) is a gorgeous record and it swells with the voice of Fontella Bass; 'All That You Give' is a shimmering lament to her late husband, Lester Bowie. Yet the music seems somehow set behind glass, held under carefully aimed lights.

For Kodwo Eshun, in *More Brilliant than the Sun*, Marley Marl's 'computerization of the Breakbeat' provided a wholly unsentimental path to the future. Its music would no longer be classical, beatless. Now, instead, 'the Futurist producer is the scientist who goes deeper into the break, who crosses the threshold of the human drummer in order to investigate the hyper dimensions of the dematerialized Breakbeat'.

For Eshun, that energy was to be found in the drum & bass of 4hero's *Parallel Universe* (1994), A Guy Called Gerald's *Black Secret Technology* (1995) and Goldie's *Timeless* (1995). Drum & bass – opaque, fast-moving, complex – seemed in tune with the coming millennium's increasing complexity: an era of innovative financial instruments, of the credit default swap and the collateralized debt obligation.

Trip-hop didn't feel like that. Trip-hop felt comforting, comfortable, even in its most sincere melancholia. Trip-hop was the loping 'Sneakin' in the Back' break, of the long spliffy inhalation seconds into Massive Attack's 'Blue Lines'. Drum & bass, famously, sliced and sped 'Amen, Brother' to almost incomprehensible degrees, its transient, silky qualities emulsified into a filmy helium supersurface above the music's plunging basslines and the break's bombastic release. Drum & bass would last into 2-step garage and on into grime and dubstep. Trip-hop would recline into lounge and downtempo.

The long interaction between hip-hop and electronic music has continued – as Laurent Fintoni's book *Redroom Beats & B-Sides* (2020) ably outlines, through three decades, and towards the LA 'beat scene' of Ras G, Georgia Anne Muldrow, Daedelus, Teebs, The Gaslamp Killer, Nosaj Thing, Thundercat, and Flying Lotus.

And – for jazz never rests – there is now a long tradition of jazz met with hip-hop and beat-driven electronic music. Chicago drummer and bandleader Makaya McCraven splices live performances into spiritual beat-collage on albums like 2018's *Universal Beings*. In the 2010s, London's jazz scene became once more an intimate communion with an audience, in venues like Buster Mantis beneath railway arches in Deptford; like Total Refreshment Centre, a former confectionary factory in Hackney. On albums like Yussef Kamaal's *Black Focus* (2016) or Emma-Jean Thackray's *Yellow* (2021) can be heard something of the West London 'broken beat' – *bruk* – sound that followed trip-hop into the early 2000s. In those years Attica Blues' Tony Nwachukwu held CDR nights at Plastic People; and there were Charlie Dark's Blacktronica nights at the ICA: 'An attempt to reclaim electronic music from its white washed arena and celebrate the contribution of black musicians to the genre.'

Recalling his mother's record collection, Dark reflected that

> like many Black kids in the seventies I took my own music for granted, thinking it would always be there, pure and undiluted for all to enjoy. Little did we know that as time went on, our beautiful music would be repackaged, re-branded and re-sold back to the very people that had helped mould, shape and create it in the first place.

This book has been an effort to foreground the artifice of categorization as a technology. It has also, perhaps, been a nostalgic invocation of a nostalgic music made of nostalgic materials.

Maybe genres drawn out of categorical wishful thinking have something inherently regressive about them: they cannot *not* be made of other things. Everything in trip-hop's formative components – hip-hop, dub, jazz – should have made it communal, forward-facing and lasting. But trip-hop was cordoned off from the genres in which it was in active dialogue – *not* dub, *not* hip-hop, *not* jazz – and so it could be isolated, artificial, nostalgic and individualistic.

Trip-hop was part of the soundtrack of those middle 1990s, when post-war consumerism was made consensus, a saturating cultural nostalgia prefatory to the years ahead of austerity and tumid inequality. It could be zany, time-wasting wankery; dull balladry; low-grade background smultz; hotel music at best, something vaguely exploitative at worst.

Yet trip-hop was at its best, even in its antic nostalgia, when it exposed the joints and overlaps and fractures of its own materials. The performative exaggeration of warped vinyl; Horace Andy's voice cast across Massive Attack's lurching horizons; DJ Shadow's obsessive crate-digging that never seemed to have any bottom; Tricky's gender theatrics; Beth Gibbons's voice crafted and stretched to extremes, DJ Krush's pneumatic inertia.

Ultimately, the sample reads the sampler, as Kodwo Eshun suggested in *More Brilliant than the Sun*. 'Listening to the breaks flare up from the unfamiliar track, each sample recognizes you. Heard in its unknown original, the beat becomes a Motion Capturer that seizes your skin memory, flashbacks your flesh'. If the act of listening for a sample revealed something in the cratedigger, perhaps so too does how we hear a genre, in us.

And so, one way to think about trip-hop is as a kind of contrast agent, a barium swallow, for complicity. We're all shortchanged, and all complicit, when we use labels that act as tools of daily erasure. Proclaiming something the new thing absolves us of the hard work of discovering – and respecting – its origins, particularly when that involved digging around for obscure 1980s instrumental hip-hop B-sides before Discogs and YouTube. Not to mention pushing yourself out of cultural perspectives and environments which you have been led to believe are natural and inevitable. Categories and labels are instruments of absolution – means to evade intellectual curiosity and avoid empathy to the lives of others. That should be a disappointing moral system, especially if you're someone for whom music is a path out of closed-mindedness.

This is not a problem that has gone away. True: almost any song is within reach – mega-platforms like Spotify, Apple Music; a lossy and hot MP3 on YouTube. The role of the critic with all their microstatus of discovery and category-naming has receded, somewhat, into the crowd. Yet the discovery algorithms of the big platforms and their authoritatively presented playlists are opaque in their design and constantly subject to change. A record-store clerk could once misshelve CDs to subvert a store's 'trip-hop' section. Now, metadata has but few authorities. The slight nudges which initiate multiplying advantages of our chaotic winner-take-all dynamics are considerably more opaque than whether a radio DJ plays your song. It's easy to see how, still today, a spontaneously crafted category – the name of a playlist, say – might obscure some artists to the advantage of others. And systems that put mere micropayments into the hands of artists aren't likely to upend the inequity in music's commercial structure.

In other words, in the age of superabundance we're no less subject to ignorance of music that requires active effort on our parts as listeners – now *users* – to address. So perhaps the responsibilities for all this have shifted – from critic, or label marketing copywriter, to listener: to us. It's on us to discern the narratives of music we like and seek.

Narratives need acts of witness; acts of memory.

In 2017, the Grenfell Tower fire in London's North Kensington held a terrifying resonance to the 1981 New Cross fire.[1] Then, dub poet Linton Kwesi Johnson had written in 'New Crass Massakah' of the Black community's rage and grief.

> how di whole a black Britn did rack wid grief
> how di whole a black Britn tun a melancally blue

Years later, asked about his album *Darker Than Blue* (2015), North London's Kwesi Darko, who records (sometimes) as Blue Daisy, said

> I'm a black individual in this world. I am darker than blue. This is the label that they put on me. I'm black. Not only am I out here fighting my demons personally, confronting them face to face, I'm also out here fighting a society or a world that still, as much as we try not to look at it that way, still perceives people of my race as lower – in the Western world, they still perceive people of my race in their own boundary.

His work includes in its influences grime, dubstep and glitch; and it recalls plainly the music of Massive Attack and Tricky. For, like them, his music is the product of the Atlantic world; and of years of recession and austerity; of resurgent racism and unrest. *The Sunday Gift* came out in 2011, a few months after riots had crisscrossed the UK in the most widespread civil disorder since 1981. It is a great smear of sound, anger, voices, and beats – chaotic, delicate, overwhelming. It invokes London's great space and a communal rebuke to the 'no such thing as society' ethos of the 2010s, just as were the massives and collectives and warehouse parties and raves to the 1980s and 1990s.

Narratives need founding figures, too, and call-backs.

For the 2014 album *Adrian Thaws*, Tricky recorded a version of Janet Kay's 'Silly Games'. The song is sublimely charming, consoling. Here, it is silkily tentative in Tirzah and Tricky's mouths – guarded, somehow; yet still it suggests something of homecoming, return.

'Silly Games' was written by Dennis Bovell who, with others, had pioneered the Lovers Rock subgenre, among his many contributions in a career of service to bass culture. Bovell is the long musical partner of Linton Kwesi Johnson; albums like 1980s' *Bass Culture* and 1984s' *Making History* suggest, in their league of bass and spoken word, an alternative precursor to the delivery of Massive Attack, including Tricky.

And Bovell produced the first album, *Y* (1979), by The Pop Group: dub and punk and musique concrète that would salt trip-hop at its edges: Tricky's music; Massive Attack's *Mezzanine*. For The Pop Group was led by Mark Stewart – who pushed Tricky onstage at the first Smith & Mighty gig.

In 2009, Bovell collaborated with Italian electronic producer Marzio Aricò on an album by Jamaican dub poet Jean Binta Breeze, *Eena Me Corner*. Bovell's basslines, Aricò's post-glitch drum programming; and Breeze's storytelling vaulting laughter and scoring witness to the psychic damage of the Atlantic world, above the music's fractured minimalism.

Essential listening

- UNKLE, *Psyence Fiction* (Mo' Wax, 1998)
- Saul Williams, *Elohim (1972)* (Big Dada, 1998)
- Rjd2, *Deadringer* (Definitive Jux, 2002)
- Rjd2, *The Horror EP* (Definitive Jux, 2003)

- Blockhead, *Music by Cavelight* (Ninja Tune, 2004)
- The Cinematic Orchestra, *Motion* (Ninja Tune, 1999)
- The Cinematic Orchestra, *Every Day* (Ninja Tune, 2002)
- Ras G, *My Kinda Blues* (Ghetto Sci-Fi Music, 2017)
- Makaya McCraven, *Universal Beings* (International Anthem, 2018)
- Blue Daisy, *The Sunday Gift* (Black Acre, 2011)
- Jean Binta Breeze, *Eena Me Corner* (Arroyo, 2009)

Also recommended

- Company Flow, *Little Johnny from the Hospitul (Breaks End Instrumentuls Vol.1)* (Rawkus, 1999)
- Omega One, *The Lo-Fi Chronicles* (Nature Sounds, 2005)
- The Cinematic Orchestra, *Man with a Movie Camera* (Ninja Tune, 2003)
- Skalpel, *Skalpel* (Ninja Tune, 2004)
- J Malik, *Slow Motion* (Infrared, 1997)
- Nosaj Thing, *Views/Octopus EP* (self-released, 2006)
- Nosaj Thing, *Drift* (Alpha Pup, 2009)
- Knxwledge, *Hud Dreems* (Stones Throw, 2015)
- Yussef Kamaal, *Black Focus* (2016)
- Emma-Jean Thackray, *Yellow* (2021)
- Blue Daisy, *Darker Than Blue* (R&S, 2015)

10 essential tracks

1. DJ Shadow, 'Midnight in a Perfect World'
2. Massive Attack, 'Teardrop'
3. Tricky, 'Aftermath – Version 1'
4. Portishead, 'Roads'
5. Björk, 'Possibly Maybe'
6. Smoke City, 'Devil Mood'
7. Attica Blues, 'Blueprint'
8. DJ Cam, 'Lost Kingdom' featuring Kakoli Sengupta
9. REQ, 'Razzamatazz'
10. Peace Orchestra, 'Who Am I'

Acknowledgements

This book depends on the works of countless writers and journalists, and of course – hopefully rendered faithfully – the words of the artists themselves. These are cited with a full list of sources at https://www.bloomsbury.com/us/triphop-9781501373602/

Key books included Stevie Chick's *Ninja Tune: 20 Years of Beats & Pieces*; Ian Bourland's *Blue Lines* and Eliot Wilder's *Endtroducing .....* in the 33 1/3 series; and Tara Rodgers's *Pink Noises: Women on Electronic Music and Sound*. Laurent Fintoni's *Bedroom Beats & B-Sides: Instrumental Hip Hop & Electronic Music At the Turn of the Century* is an excellent overview; and his reporting on the Illbient scene was invaluable.

Essential to various parts of this book were *Dub: Soundscapes and Shattered Songs in Jamaican Reggae* by Michael E. Veal; *Bass, Mids, Tops: An Oral History of Soundsystem Culture* by Joe Muggs and Brian David Stevens; Lloyd Bradley's *Sounds Like London: 100 Years of Black Music in the Capital* and Caspar Melville's *It's a London Thing: How Rare Groove, Acid House and Jungle Remapped the City*; Phil Johnson's *Straight Outa Bristol: Massive Attack, Portishead, Tricky and the Roots of Trip-Hop*; Nate Patrin's *Bring That Beat Back: How Sampling Built Hip-Hop*; and Michael Denning's *Noise Uprising: The Audiopolitics of a World Musical Revolution*.

The 2018 Matthew Jones–directed documentary *The Man From Mo' Wax* was also extremely helpful, as was the monograph *Urban Archaeology: Twenty-One Years of Mo' Wax*.

Several fan sites and archives were particularly helpful, including Moon Palace, Red Lines, the unofficial Mo' Wax

Discography, Dale Cooper's Mo'Wax Please and James Gaunt's Mo'Wax: Where Are They Now series.

Research from my earlier book on Portishead's *Dummy* obviously informed this volume, including incredibly helpful interviews with Dave McDonald, Tim Saul and Zeid Hamden. I am also grateful to Wai Wan for his insight into the Manchester scene and his own album *Distraction*.

My thanks to everyone at Bloomsbury for their support and great patience as I grappled with something as shapeless as trip-hop: Leah Babb-Rosenfeld, Amy Martin, Rachel Moore, Elizabeth Kellingley, Rebecca Morofsky, Joanna McDowall and Louise Dugdale.

And to the unceasingly kind and unsparingly insightful Annie Zaleski for helping me find the shape in it.

For their early thoughts on this book and great support throughout: Anshuman Iddamsetty, Alison Little and Anupa Mistry. And to Mike Denney, who introduced me to so much of this music in the first place.

To my parents, Rosemary and Jim, for their love and support.

And to Niharika, for encouraging me at the beginning and at the end; for reading bits of this late at night and for hearing out the takes that (thank you) didn't even end up in the book; for the reality checks; for having my back and being at my side. At times this thing seemed impossible, but you knew it wasn't, and so I made it.

Notes

Chapter 2

1 In the United States it was denied a release until 2019.

2 Not to be confused with its distant step-child, the 'drum & bass' genre, which was an evolution from the ragga-infused post-hardcore breakbeat 'jungle' music.

3 Did the 'trip' of trip-hop acknowledge the role that many – including Lee Perry and Scientist – attributed to the use of marijuana in the development of dub, thereby duly crediting the dub innovators? No.

Chapter 3

1 Paul Johnson – brother of Wild Bunch's Miles – dissented: 'there was absolutely no conversation across the social boundaries and the melting pot thing is an illusion'.

Chapter 4

1 Including Phuture's DJ Pierre, Earl 'Spanky' Smith and Herb J.

Chapter 5

1 Strictly Kev would also assume art design responsibilities for the label, cementing its quality graphic design and multimedia approach.

Chapter 6

1 Peterson remembers it being 'Iron Leg' by Mickey & the Soul Generation, 'a rare groove record with a mad rock guitar intro and no beat. I started vary speeding it so it sounded all warped.'

2 Like Massive Attack's 'Blue Lines' sampling Tom Scott and the L.A. Express's 'Sneakin' in the Back'.

3 Vibert's Wagon Christ identity is closest to trip-hop: breakbeats, mostly slower tempos, mood architecture drawn of jazzy keyboards.

4 Even though the *Birth of the Cool* sessions featured as many Black musicians as white – including, of course, Miles Davis, under whose name Capitol compiled the music in 1957.

5 Or, in hindsight, might only be interested in listening for potential samples.

Chapter 9

1 Willner's own *Whoops I'm an Indian*, released on Howie B's Pussyfoot label in 1998, sounds like a William Vollmann book; it sounds like a sort of accursed American sibling to the

Avalanches' glistening and blissful Aussie surfpop sample-fest *Since I Left You* (2000).

2   In 1944 Burroughs and Kerouac were arrested as material witnesses in the murder of David Kammerer by Lucien Carr; Kerouac helped him dispose of the murder weapon.

Chapter 10

1   Illbient is often seen as a parallel sub-genre to trip-hop, and is certainly deserving of its own study. Laurent Fintoni's interviews and reporting have preserved an important record.

Chapter 14

1   Jay Bernard's devastating 2019 poem *Surge* explicitly connects the two events.